Jihad in Islam

Ayatullah Ne'matollah Salehi Najafabadi

Translated by Dr. Hamid Mavani

Organization for the Advancement of Islamic Knowledge
and Humanitarian Services
(O.A.I.K. & H.S.)
Montreal, Quebec
Canada

Jihad in Islam
Ayatullah Ne'matollah Salehi Najafi

Translated by Dr. Hamid Mavani

Published by
Organization for the Advancement of Islamic Knowledge and
Humanitarian Services
(O.A.I.K. & H.S.)
P. O. Box 786
Station H
Montreal, Quebec
H3G 2M7
Canada

ISBN 978-0-9680868-5-8

Contents

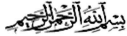

In the Name of God, the Infinitely Kind, the All Merciful

Translator's Introduction

Any study of jihad is fraught with difficulties, especially in the post-9/11 context, because Muslim apologists and their sympathizers' sources and findings, tailored to a predominantly non-Muslim audience, are diametrically opposed to those of the hostile polemicists who associate jihad with violence and militancy. The former insist that jihad is primarily a spiritual struggle against the self (*jihad al-nafs*) and its evil inclinations, although they acknowledge that it may take the military form of self-defense when, and only when, Muslims face an aggressive enemy. This group argues that the Islamic concept of jihad has been "hijacked" by the extremists and terrorists, who have transformed it into a murderous weapon to kill innocent civilians. These violent individuals cannot represent its spiritual reality testified to in the Qur'an and the hadith literature,[1] as an essentially nonviolent activity. Hostile polemicists view jihad as nothing short of an offensive war firmly rooted in, sanctioned, and encouraged by the Qur'an, the hadith, and juridical rulings (*fatwas*); an offensive war that has the

---

[1] The latter source consists of the Prophet's sayings (*qawl*), actions (*fiʿl*), and tacit approval (*taqrir*), as well as those of his Companions in Sunni Islam and of the infallible Imams in Shiʿi Islam, who are viewed as extensions and continuation of his prophetic authority and personality since they have inherited his knowledge and charisma.

sole purpose of gaining global dominance by imposing Islam and expanding the territorial sphere of Islamdom. This model is, according to them, clearly reflected in the wars of expansion and conquest after the Prophet's death.

Both perspectives contain an element of truth that can be supported by a selective retrieval and disregard of evidence from the sources, and/or by those engaged in processes of reductionism and decontextualization: one aspires to sanitize Muslim history and to spiritualize jihad as exclusively and inherently a nonviolent activity, while the other attempts to conceptualize its normative expression as essentially militant and violent. The information that can be gleaned from the early sources is conflicting and contradictory, especially when one compares it with the comprehensive Qur'anic worldview. Understood in the spirit of its entirety, this worldview envisions military jihad as an abhorrent and distasteful last resort; in the realm of hadith and jurisprudence (*fiqh*), however, jurists regard it as a divinely rewarded annual activity designed to force the non-Muslims to convert. I explored this tension in an article that appeared in the *Journal of Shi'a Islamic Studies* (JSIS) in autumn 2011, which JSIS has graciously allowed me to reproduce in the appendix. I am indebted to Dr. Amir Dastmalchian and Mr. Hamid Tehrani for granting me the necessary permission to do so.

I argue that the expansionist theology that can be gleaned from the intolerant hadiths and juridical rulings was informed by the Muslim community's existing sociopolitical situation, and formulated within its concrete experiences at a time when both its territory and hegemony were on the rise. In other words, those *fatwas* which legitimated such offensive wars were a function of historical specificity. Although a holistic reading of the Qur'an completely undermines this position, a case can be made for it if one decontextualizes certain verses and then imposes a particular hermeneutics upon them. Given that the Qur'an views the freedom of religion and conscience as an inalienable and fundamental right, initiating a war under the pretense of wanting to remove impediments in the way of people so that they could become familiar with the true message of Islam and/or to extend the abode of Islam cannot be justified. Even the sole Qur'anic allowance for war, self-defense, is cancelled once the enemy agrees to a truce and a cessation of hostilities. In other words, non-Muslims cannot be attacked just because of their disbelief (*kufr*).

The work in your hand is a translation of Ayatullah Salehi Najafabadi's (d. 2006) Persian-language *Jihad der Islam*. Born in 1923 in Najafabad, Iran, he studied under several eminent scholars, including Ayatullah Sayyid Husayn Boroujerdi (d. 1961) and 'Allamah Sayyid Muhammad Husayn Tabataba'i (d. 1981). He was an original, systematic, and uniquely gifted intellectual who authored a number of works on different topics, some of them quite controversial and sensitive. One such work, which received a disproportionate amount of attention is his *Shahid-e javid* (*Eternal Martyr*), published in 1968 with an introduction by Ayatullah Husayn 'Ali Montazeri (d.

2009). In this work, he offers a novel and radically different interpretation of the Karbala episode and Imam Husayn's mission: what happened there was not divinely preordained, and the Imam did not have foreknowledge of the events which would climax in the martyrdom of him and his small band of followers. This suggestion raised serious protests among the clergy; yet, he also received support and endorsement from some prominent jurists.

In this work, Ayatullah Najafabadi tackles the controversial concept of jihad with candor and scholarly rigor, by citing the Qur'an as the criterion and standard for evaluating the validity (or lack thereof) of the various hadith reports and legal rulings on this subject. His strategy of invoking the Qur'an as the arbitrator and the evaluation metric by which to assess the legal rulings' soundness is quite understandable, because he is writing as an insider of the faith tradition with its attendant presuppositions, assumptions, and premises. He provides cogent arguments and sound proofs from reliable sources to refute the claim made by the overwhelming majority of classical and contemporary Sunni and Shi'i jurists that the Qur'an, hadiths, and past juridical precedents have legitimated unconditional warfare against unbelievers, even if the latter are seeking peace and are non-hostile. This is so because the ultimate aim is to convert all non-Muslims except the People of the Book, who have been grudgingly accepted as protected minorities as long as they pay the poll tax (*jizyah*), and are humbled into accepting Islam's supremacy, and the Islamic state's dominion. This conception clearly violates the Prophet's practice and the unconditional Qur'anic verse that says, "There is no compulsion in religion: true guidance has become distinct from error" (Q. 2:256). Since force and coercion automatically invalidate one's free will and human agency, no act performed thereafter would merit any praise or reward, because only the correctness of one's intention (*niyyah*) can determine its validity and moral worth.

The reader must keep in mind that Ayatullah Najafabadi's arguments are addressed primarily to Muslims living in a culture where many aspects of their religion are taken for granted and thus do not need to be verified. Furthermore, he is writing in a language that lends itself to elaborate explanations, examples, and repetitions that could irritate astute western readers. As such, I have taken the liberty of removing many such repetitions and, at times, succinctly summarizing his lengthy elaborations, without distorting his work or the flow of his arguments. Finally, I did not translate chapter 3, which deals with prisoners of war, because it was not the main focus of his work and was only tangentially related to its stated objectives.

It is my distinct pleasure to offer my thanks to those who have been instrumental in actualizing this project: my wife Mahbubeh Ettehadi, for her invaluable assistance and patience in translating this work, as Persian is her native language; her brother Shahram, for tapping his creative mind and crafting several designs for the book cover and the back page; and a remarkable and selfless anonymous donor, for the generous grant which made it possible to bring this translation project to fruition. May God shower them all with His choicest blessings. Amen.

I have used M. A. S. Abdel Haleem's translation of the Qur'an throughout this work with minor modifications, if warranted. The upper case "I" in the word "Imam" is used to refer to the infallible Imam in Shi'ism, whereas the smaller case "i" is employed in its lexical meaning of a leader (*imam*) in some minor or major capacity. Finally, all the dates are given in the Common Era (CE).

I hope that this translated work on jihad will partially compensate for the lack of accessible and reliable English-language literature on this potent and volatile subject. The author's nuanced and sophisticated treatment of this subject matter, along with the diversity of interpretations contained in it, will, in all likelihood, lead one to conclude with humility that there is no essentialist and monolithic understanding or interpretation of any topic and, as such, no claim can be made of having attained a "true," "authentic," "original," or "pure" reading of anything.

wa bi 'l-lahi 't-tawfiq

Dr. Hamid Mavani
Claremont Graduate University
School of Religion
Claremont, California

June 23, 2012 / Sha'ban 3, 1433

Author's Preface

On my visit to the war front during the days of Iraq's imposed war on Iran, I witnessed heart-rending scenes of the martyrs and the wounded being removed from the battlefield. With the totality of my being, I experienced the bitter and excruciatingly painful casualties of war. At that juncture, the necessity of investigating the subject of jihad from the perspective of the Qur'an, hadith, and jurisprudential writings to discover the real truth about it suddenly dawned on me.

Upon my return to Qum, I sought to make this subject the primary material for study in the advanced classes (*dars-e kharij*) on *ijtihad*. Accordingly, an announcement was made that these classes would be offered at the Masjid-e imam. A total of seventy-three sessions were developed, and received with great enthusiasm, under the rubric of jihad.

During this investigation, I concluded that the portrayals of jihad in the Qur'an and the Prophet's practice, on the one hand, and the jurists' legal works, on the other, are poles apart and stand in sharp contrast to each other. The core reason for this striking disparity is the jurists' contention that the primary form of jihad is that of an offensive war designed to impose Islam on non-believers through military force, even if they are non-hostile and pose no threat. Moreover, according to them, this constitutes a divine responsibility similar to the obligation of fasting and ritual prayer, even though the Qur'an and the Prophet require Muslims to have cordial relations with the unbelievers and to be kind toward the harmless: "He does not forbid you to deal kindly and justly with anyone who has not fought you for your faith or driven you out of your homes: God loves the just ones" (Q. 60:8). Furthermore, the Qur'an prohibits pursuing a war once the unbelievers agree on a truce, or stop fighting: "So if they withdraw and do not fight you, and offer you peace, then God gives you no way against them" (Q. 4:90).

Here we see the great disparity between what the jurists have written, and what the Qur'an and the Prophet's practice proclaim. Westerners have taunted and derided Muslims on the basis of what is recorded in their jurisprudential books, claiming that Islam is a bloodthirsty religion which advocates unprovoked offensive war to bring to fruition its vision of overpowering all non-believers and forcing them to convert. It is the jurists' onerous responsibility to dispel such stereotypes and misunderstandings by revisiting their books, aligning them with the Qur'an and the Prophet's practices, and discarding all that conflicts with these two sources. By this method, jihad's true humanistic face will ultimately be displayed to humanity.

Offered below are a few instances of unsound legal rulings:

1. Imam Shafi'i argues that all Qur'anic verses that condition fighting the unbelievers upon their initiation of war have been abrogated by the verse, "Fight them until there is no more *fitnah*" (Q. 2:193). As a consequence, attacking even harmless and non-hostile unbelievers is mandatory, because the goal is to make Islam dominant. This legal ruling gradually became the norm, and was readily accepted almost without any exception by such Sunni and Shi'i scholars as Ibn Homam Hanafi, Shaykh Tusi, Ibn Idris, 'Allamah Hilli, Shahid II, Sahib Jawahir, and Ayatullah Khu'i. However, any claim of consensus on this matter, in my estimation, is incorrect and unacceptable. I will elaborate on this in the book.

2. Shi'i jurists have insisted that since only the infallible Imam can declare jihad, during his occultation this obligation is suspended. These scholars have equated the term "just ruler" (*imam 'adil*), which is mentioned in the hadiths, to the infallible Imam (*imam ma'sum*). But this understanding is incorrect, for the obligatory jihad mentioned in the Qur'an and the Prophet's practice has not been suspended.

3. Their assertion that the Prophet executed a surprise offensive attack against the Banu Mustaliq and eradicated them is incorrect.

4. Their assertion that the Prophet attacked the people of Ta'if with a mangonel and destroyed their houses while they were still inside them is incorrect.

5. Their assertion that the Prophet customarily invited unbelievers to Islam and then attacked them if they refused to do so is false. Furthermore, it contradicts his character.

6. Their ruling that it is obligatory to fight the unbelievers at least once a year is incorrect. Rather, Muslims are ordered to defend themselves whenever the unbelievers initiate war.

7. They have ruled that Muslims were initially obliged to resist the unbelievers if their ratio to the unbelievers was at least one to ten. Later on, this ruling was abrogated, and the ratio was reduced to one Muslim to two unbelievers. Consequently, defense is not obligatory if there are more than twice as many enemies than Muslims, even if it exceeds by only one person. This is incorrect, for self-defense is mandatory regardless of whether the invading enemy's numbers are double, or more, or less.

8. Shi'i jurists state that the rebels (*bughat*) are those who revolt against the infallible Imam, and that fighting them is conditional upon his directive. Based on this, during the Imam's occultation there

can be no *bughat*. But this is not a correct opinion, because even during the occultation there will be *bughat*, and Muslims will still be obliged to defend themselves. Thus, fighting rebels does not depend upon the infallible Imam's consent.

9. They say that the prisoners of war captured during the battle, but not after the battle ends, must be massacred. However, this is an incorrect opinion because the ruling on both situations is the same and it is certainly not to kill them.

I expect from those who are capable of offering constructive criticism of my work, to not instantly deny and reject whatever conflicts with their own beliefs without first rereading it with greater reflection and discernment. If after having done that they still find my opinion unacceptable, I welcome their critique, for this would be a step in the direction of perfection and the completion of knowledge.

Nematollah Salehi Najafabadi
11 Shahrivar 1382 / 2 September 2003
Tehran

Chapter 1

Is the Norm War or Peace?

The Qur'anic usage of *jihad*, in both its conventional and customary meanings, is broader than that of *qital*, for it includes all kinds of efforts and endeavors undertaken to achieve one's objective. Therefore, one can determine whether the effort expended is in the path of good or of evil only by examining the objective's context. In Q. 22:78, "Strive hard (*jahidu*) **for God** (*fi-l-lah*) as is His due;" *fi-l-lah* is an indicator suggesting that the effort is in the path of goodness. In Q. 31:15, "But if they strive (*jahada*) **to make you associate** (*'ala an tushrik*) with Me anything about which you have no knowledge," *'ala an tushrik* is an indicator signifying that the effort is in the path of evil. For the purpose of this book, we will be analyzing this term in its technical sense, i.e. "war in the path of God," which is narrower in scope than its etymological meaning.

Before we launch into a discussion on the essence of jihad, we must pose and seek to answer two questions:

1. Does Islam allow Muslims to go to war for the purpose of imposing their religion?

2. Is peace the norm when invaded by an enemy? Upon repelling the aggressor and forcing it to

surrender, must efforts be undertaken to end to the war and establish a truce? Or is war a norm that demands continued expansion until it gradually reaches its maximum capacity?

Question 1:

According to Islam, going to war for the purpose of forcing Islam upon others is not permissible, because "There is no compulsion in religion: true guidance has become distinct from error" (Q. 2:256). At the theoretical level, this "abstract" (*khabari*) sentence is actually a "concrete" (*insha'i*) sentence with practical applications in a particular context. The statement "there is no compulsion in religion" means that no force or duress must be used while inviting someone to Islam because truth and falsehood are discernable by the conscience and human instinct and, as such, there is no need for force. Therefore compulsion, be it by threats or warfare, should not be invoked in the matter of religion or creed.

In other words, belief, essentially a matter of the heart, cannot be attained through force because human beings only accept that which is dictated by their conscience (*fitrah*). Force does not change anyone's belief or bring about a new and fresh belief, and thus employing it is pointless. Given this reality, Islam prohibits engaging in war for the sake of imposing Islam.

Question 2:

Peace is the norm even when the Muslims are confronted with an enemy invasion, on the premise that war is the outcome of a specific necessity and invoked only after the Muslims have been attacked. After the latter's defeat, however, there is no need for it. The Qur'an therefore states that a war ends when the aggressors have been defeated and their ensuing sedition removed: "Fight them until there is no more persecution [*fitnah*], and [your] worship is devoted to God" (Q. 2:193). If it is said that "the word *fitnah* in the verse is used in the context of eradicating persecution and connotes a universal applicability, thereby suggesting that one should continue to fight until there is absolutely no sedition present in the world, not just the sedition that the invading enemy has brought into being," then the reply would be: "Based on the context of the previous verse, 'if they do fight you, kill them' (Q. 2:92), war is conditional upon the enemy's aggression." Here, what is intended is a special kind of sedition caused by the enemy's assault. Clearly, Q. 2:193 has two objectives: removing sedition and the evil brought about by the enemy. As soon as these objectives are achieved, fighting must end and a truce must be negotiated and enforced. In actuality, this particular verse is saying that "you should fight against the enemy that has attacked you and uproot the source of the sedition so that the war will end and a truce can be implemented."

The "Chapter of Battle Gains" (*Surah al-Anfal*) contains an important section related to the Battle of Badr: "But if they incline towards peace, you [Prophet] must also incline towards it, and put your trust in God" (Q. 8:61). Before this verse, Muslims are instructed to "Prepare whatever forces you can muster, including war horses, to frighten off God's enemies and yours" (Q. 8:60). Five verses later, the Prophet is ordered to "urge the believers to fight" (Q. 8:65). In between these verses on war, God commands: "But if they incline towards peace, you [O Prophet] must also incline towards it, and put your trust in God" (Q. 8:61). In other words, if the enemy, even in the midst of war, shows its preference for peace, then you should accept it. Thus, one would be correct in saying that Islam regards peace and reconciliation as foundational in any social concourse, and that one should strive for and attempt to preserve these ideals.

Taking the foundational and essential meaning of war into account, one could say that if the unbelievers were to adopt a position of peace and mutual co-existence at all times vis-à-vis the Muslims, then there would never be a cause for war. This is because the passage Q. 8:60-65 contains no exceptions when it comes to matters of peace and co-existence. The Messenger of God and his followers are obligated to aspire for peace and never to initiate war against the unbelievers.

Peace is the natural state of society

Just as the body's well-being is the natural state for every human being and sickness is an accidental one, peace and serenity are society's natural state and war is viewed as an accidental state. Q. 8:61 refers to this as well: peace and a life of repose and comfort are society's natural states, and thus one must strive to preserve them. If the invading enemy shows any inclination toward peace, then it must be accepted and welcomed so that society, freed from the disease of war, can be restored to a healthy state.

The side that initiates confrontation and disturbs the social peace is judged to be wrong. In principle, the human conscience dislikes initiating an attack against another and considers it to be unjust and unjustifiable. From this perspective, wherever a war breaks out an attempt is made to discover which side initiated it. This is done to determine who is to be blamed when the war is over and to publicize this indictment throughout the area, region, and the world. This shows that initiating war, for whatever reason, is against human conscience even if it is invoked in the name of religion.

Doing good to the unbelievers

At times, some religious people state that doing good to those who follow a different belief is improper. Such an opinion has been present in Muslim society, both now and in the past, even though the Qur'an condemns it. In fact, the Qur'an warns Muslims that God expects them to be benevolent and just to the unbelievers, provided they are not harassing Muslims: "And He does not forbid you to deal kindly and justly with anyone who has not fought you for your faith or driven you out of your homes: God loves the just" (Q. 60:8). Clearly, Islam desires to instill purity, goodness, and respect for all human beings within the souls of its followers, for these qualities soften everyone's hearts and enable them to begin laying the foundation for societal peace and harmony. This is evidence that peace, according to Islam, is the underpinning and basis for a truly Islamic society. There is only one exception: befriending unbelievers after they have militarily attacked the Muslims. In such a situation, Muslims are obliged to expel them from their land. Any friendship under such conditions would enable the unbelievers to gain a foothold in Muslim society, which would result in colossal harm. As the "Chapter of Women Tested" (*Surah al-Mumtahana*) proclaims: "But God forbids you to take as allies those who have fought against you for your faith, driven you out of your homes, and helped others to drive you out: any of you who take them as allies will truly be wrongdoers" (Q. 60:9).

Question: Keeping in mind what has been said so far, that imposing Islam through warfare is not allowed and that peace is foundational and the norm for which one should strive and then preserve, what is jihad and when can Muslims fight the unbelievers? To answer these questions, it is necessary to analyze the relevant Qur'anic verses.

Qur'anic verses on war and jihad

Verses related to fighting the unbelievers can be divided into two groups: (1) those that specify the conditions and limitations of war and (2) those that are unconditional and absolute because no conditions or limitations are set out.

First category: Conditional verses

1. "Fight in God's cause against those who fight you, but do not overstep the limits (*la ta'tadu*): God does not love those who overstep the limits" (Q. 2:190).

Several important points are made here:

(a) War must be waged in the path of God and for Him only. Those waging it cannot be driven by territorial expansion, vengeance, lust for power, desire for hegemony and supremacy over others, and similar motives. *In God's cause* means the path of goodness that is in humanity's best interest, that which will earn His approval and satisfaction (e.g., liberating a place so that its inhabitants can establish a life that will benefit them in this life and the hereafter; defending the oppressed and destroying the oppressive aggressors, the source of sedition and corruption, who have replaced the inhabitants' freedom with injustice, force, and a stifling, suffocating environment).

(b) This verse says to fight "against those who fight you." Accordingly, if there is no enemy attack there can be no war. This limitation was imposed to make war permissible. If there is no aggression, no form of offensive war is permissible.

(c) This verse prohibits any form of transgression and attack, as generally understood (e.g., killing women and children, burning houses and farm lands, unnecessary cutting of trees, and massacring captives). The meaning of transgression and aggression is vividly clear, and one's conscience and instinct can specify their applicability. Thus, this verse is considered absolute and unconditional and beyond the need for any interpretation.

Of course the atmosphere of war is quite inflammatory, and sometimes some people become agitated or passionate when caught up in it. In such circumstances, they may exceed the limits of justice and fairness and commit prohibited deeds. This is why the Qur'an warns the decision-makers, general commanders, and soldiers not to transgress the limits when engaging the enemy.

Incidentally, one commentator on this verse remarks that *la ta'tadu* means "do not attack those who have not attacked you and do not initiate war, for this would constitute transgression and exceeding the limits." On the basis of this statement, the phrase *wa la ta'tadu* is an emphatic imperative meant to corroborate and confirm the limitation that Muslims can fight only "against those who fight you." Thus, one who has not been attacked has no right to initiate war.[2]

(d) This verse reminds the soldiers of Islam, after prohibiting them from exceeding the limits, that God does not love the transgressors. In other words, a Muslim fighting in God's path and for His satisfaction should know that exceeding the boundaries of justice and fairness on the battlefield and engaging in what is prohibited will cause him/her to lose His love. Thus, transgression invites God's anger and, accordingly, such people will be the recipients of God's wrath.

Given that Islam has enshrined jihad for the sake of uprooting oppression and excess, as well as for enlivening justice and fairness, God obviously cannot accept that which contradicts these two goals.

---

[2]Hasan al-Tabrisi, *Majma' al-bayan fi tafsir al-Qu'an*, exegesis on Qur'an, 2:190.

2. "Kill them wherever you encounter them, and drive them out from where they drove you out, for persecution is more serious than killing. Do not fight them at the Sacred Mosque unless they fight you there. If they do fight you, kill them – this is what such disbelievers deserve" (Q. 2:191).

This is the second verse that places limits and conditions on war. The pronoun in *kill them* refers to the previous verse *against those who fight you,* and its meaning is "removing the evil of the aggressive unbelievers who initiated war is possible by killing them." It then says: "Do not fight them at the Sacred Mosque unless they fight you therein. If they do fight you, kill them – this is what such disbelievers deserve."

This verse contains several important points.

(a) Muslims, when facing the unbelievers who have initiated the war and seek their annihilation, have the right to defend themselves by killing these invaders wherever they find them, because this is the only way to remove their evil.

(b) Muslims are prohibited from initiating war. There is, however, one exception: self-defense.

(c) This verse, addressed to those Muslims who had been expelled from Makkah by the unbelievers, is letting them know that they are entitled to do the same to the latter. This constitutes a form of self-defense.

(d) This verse states that the sedition initiated by the unbelievers, along with torturing and robbing the Makkan Muslims and preparing an army to attacks Madinah's Muslims, were more intense and destructive than their being killed by the Muslims.

(e) The permissibility of killing the unbelievers is the recompense for their initiation of the war and shedding Muslim blood. Therefore, this constitutes a just penalty.

Note: Some say that *fitnah* in Q. 2:191 and 2:193 means *shirk* (polytheism). Shaykh Muhammad 'Abduh (d. 1905), however, said that "this is contrary to the contextual exegesis of the verse."[3] In the author's estimation, this is a correct interpretation because 2:190 says "against those who fight you." The general tenor of this verse and the one coming right after it demonstrates that the unbelievers pressured the Muslims, tortured those who were in

---

[3] Muhammad Rashid Rida, *Tafsir al-Qur'an al-hakim al-shahir bi al-Tafsir al-Manar* (Beirut: Dar al-ma'rifah, 1971-), 2:210.

Makkah, and sometimes even killed them. The ones in Madinah were confronted with an unsought war, which constitutes both sedition and tribulation. Q. 2:193 proclaims: "Fight them until there is no more persecution." In other words, once the unbelievers are defeated they would be unable to impose sedition, tribulation, and war on the Muslims. 'Abdallah b. 'Umar relates: "During the time of the Prophet, the unbelievers used to imprison, torture, and kill the Muslims because of their religion. As a result, we fought them until Islam acquired strength and *fitnah* was eliminated."[4] This narration confirms that, given the verse's context, *fitnah* is to be understood as the tribulation and punishment imposed upon the Muslims by the unbelievers.

In addition, such warfare does not remove the unbelievers' *shirk,* because this belief system is rooted in the heart. As such, their military defeat neither impacts nor changes their faith, for only discussion and the presentation of proofs designed to convince them of their error can accomplish that particular goal. Thus, even when the military is defeated the unbelievers are allowed to retain their traditional faith. As a result, it is not correct to say that Muslims were directed to fight against the unbelievers to force them to discard their traditional belief system.

---

[4] Ibid., 9:666.

Linguistic meaning of *fitnah*

The root *f-t-n* means "placing gold in the heat until the pure and the impure become distinguishable." The verse, "For those who persecute (*fatanu*) believing men and women" (Q. 85:10), refers to those who burned the believers as well as the people of hellfire: "On a Day when they will be punished (*yuftanun*) by the Fire, 'Taste the punishment (*fitnah*), this is what you wished to hasten'" (Q. 51:13-14). In other words, swallow the punishment. In, "Beware of discord (*fitnah*) that harms not only the wrongdoers among you" (8:25), *fitnah* indicates tribulation and anxiety. Mahmud al-Zamakhshari (d. 1144) says that "*fitnah* has been used here to mean war, such that when it says that 'there is *fitnah* between them' it means 'war between them.'"[5]

Generally, in all cases the use of derivatives from *f-t-n* connotes difficulty. In the case of *fitnah,* the meaning of test and trial is also added. Since *shirk* contains no sense of difficulty, it cannot be the equivalent of *fitnah*. It is highly likely that those who favored such an equivalence opined that jihad is equivalent to imposing Islam by military force and could not accept that it was no more than a method of self-defense. From this perspective, they have argued that, "kill them until there is no more *fitnah*" (Q. 2:193) means that Muslims can initiate war against the unbelievers to uproot all non-Islamic belief

---

[5] Mahmud b. 'Umar al-Zamakhshari, *Asas al-balaghah* (Beirut: Dar al-sadir, 1965), 334.

systems. That is, the very existence of *shirk* makes launching an offensive war obligatory. As a result, they have undertaken *ijtihad* (scholarly research) on the word *shirk* itself. But they have done so on the basis of a pre-set meaning that they had imposed on jihad, whereas the correct method is to consult linguists, given that there is no scope for *ijtihad* on such issues. Thus, one ought not to interpret *fitnah* as *shirk*.

3. "Fight them until there is no more persecution, and [your] worship is devoted to God. If they cease hostilities, there can be no [further] hostility, except towards aggressors" (Q. 2:193).

This verse makes it clear that Muslims cannot kill unbelievers who have ended their attack. In this verse, *qatilu* is referential (*'atf*) to *qatilu* in 2:190, and the pronoun *hum* (them) in this verse refers to the same group as in Q. 2:190: "those who fight against you." One must note that Q. 2:190 instructs Muslims to fight against the aggressors and the initiators of war who, as such, fully deserve their "just reward." Q. 2:193 says: "Fight against them until there is no more *fitnah* and the *din* is for God." One of the meanings of *din* is "supremacy" or "domination and control." The contextual meaning is as follows: those unbelievers who have the capability to attack Muslims also have the power to control Muslims. When they are defeated by the Muslims' self-defensive counterattack, however, they lose their supremacy and control and must submit to the Muslims' dominion and God's supremacy.

This verse cites two legitimate reasons for bringing the war to an end: (1) the utter destruction of the aggressive unbelievers and (2) to force them to accept their defeat. In other words, the command to fight aggressive unbelievers in these verses, like the two preceding ones, is limited to a war of self-defense.

4. "Those who have been attacked are permitted to take up arms because they have been wronged – God has the power to help them – those who have been driven unjustly from their homes only for saying, 'Our Lord is God.' If God did not repel some people by means of others, many monasteries, churches, synagogues, and mosques, where God's name is much invoked, would have been destroyed. God is sure to help those who help His cause – God is strong and mighty" (Q. 22:39-40).

Here, the Qur'an specifies that war is permissible and can be pursued if the enemy initiates the aggression and subjects the people to oppression and suffering. In this situation, they not only have the right, but the obligation to defend themselves. It is self-evident that if the enemy commits no aggression, the Muslims cannot initiate war against people who desire peace and a life of non-violence. Moreover, they cannot be attacked under the guise of imposing religion, because: "There is no compulsion in the matter of religion" (Q. 2:256). The next verse signals that people who were unjustly expelled from their homeland, only because of their belief in God, have this right of self-defense. Specifically, this refers to the emigrant Muslims of Makkah who were tortured and underwent suffering at the hands of the unbelievers and were forced to migrate.

This verse comments on what had happened and reminds the people of the difficult situation of the Muslim emigrants forced to flee to Yathrib (Madinah's pre-Islamic name). However, the intent is not to suggest that such self-defense is conditional upon being expelled from one's place by an attack, thereby precluding other situations where self-defense could be invoked.

This verse lists some of the negative outcomes of not engaging in self-defense: the spread of corruption and destruction of synagogues, churches, and mosques. Here, permission to launch a defensive war is equated to defense in the path of God by allowing oppressed people to participate in jihad. This empowers the warriors to confront the aggressors and, as a result of the latter's defeat, to remove their evil. Accordingly, the context of defense here is a legally mandated (*tashri'i*) jihad, as opposed to that of creative authority (*takwini*). This conclusion can be derived from, "God is sure to help those who help His cause" (Q. 22:40), which is compatible and appropriate in this situation. Therefore, "helping God" means implementing His commands and that whoever does so has actually helped Him. Thus, He will help those who implement the directive on jihad to overpower the enemy.

Accordingly, those exegetes who have interpreted self-defense as *takwini* (i.e., "God removes tribulations because of the blessings of the virtuous") seem to be mistaken, for this definition is not in line with the verse's primary focus: God permits the oppressed to engage in self-defense so that they can remove the aggressor's evil. Thus, the verse cannot mean that God neutralizes the tribulations which would have transpired as a result of the people having ignored their prayers, zakat, and pilgrimage, as stated in *Majma' al-bayan*'s commentary of Q. 2:251. In addition, this pedagogy is faulty because it indirectly encourages and invites one to neglect these very obligations.

If the verse is interpreted as the disobedient are protected and safeguarded by the grace of the virtuous, then it would have been written as "*wa law la daf'u Allahi bi ba'd al-nasi 'an ba'd*," instead of, "*wa law la daf'u Allahi al-nasa ba'duhum bi ba'd*" because *daf'*, when joined with *'an*, becomes transitive and conveys the meaning of safeguarding, as in: "God will defend the believers (*inna Allaha yudafi'u 'an al-ladhina amanu*)" (Q. 22:38). But if the verb is reflexive, it conveys the meaning of repelling something, as in: "Repel evil with good" (Q. 23:96). *Al-sayyi'ah* is the object of *idfa'*, namely, repel the bad by a method that is better. In "*wa law la daf' al-nasa*" (Q. 22:40), the word *daf'* is reflexive and its object is *al-nas*. Moreover, it does not convey the sense of protection or safeguarding, for here it means, "to make something distant." As such, the interpretation of Q. 2:251

mentioned above does not accord with the verse and thus must be rejected.

Another point is that the verse mentions no relationship between the conditions and the recompense. If the underlying idea here is that God, in the absence of the blessings of the virtuous, would not remove the tribulations and thus allow the places of worship to be destroyed, then one has to question the logical relationship between what is being inferred: not removing the tribulations from the wrong-doers and the destruction of sacred places? Rather, God's bringing of destruction upon the evil ones protects the sacred places from their evil.

5. "A sacred month for a sacred month: violation of sanctity [calls for] fair retribution. So if anyone commits aggression against you, attack him as he attacked you, but be mindful of God, and know that He is with those who are mindful of Him" (Q. 2:194).

This verse is held to be related to the incident of Hudaybiyyah (628). The Makkan polytheists did not allow the Prophet and the Muslims to perform 'umrah (lesser pilgrimage) and attacked them with swords and stones. Eventually, a truce was reached: The Muslims would return to Madinah without performing the pilgrimage, but could come again at the same time next year and spend three days in the city. The following year, the Prophet and the Muslims left for Makkah, again in

Dhulqaʿdah (one of the sacred months) to perform ʿumrah. Hasan al-Tabrisi (d. 1153) says that the polytheists of Makkah were thinking of launching a surprise attack on the Muslims. As a result, this verse was revealed to remind the Muslims that even though no fighting is allowed during the sacred months, they can defend themselves if the unbelievers attack them. If this is the case, there is no penalty for violating this tradition.[6] As a result, this verse presents a general rule: When confronted with an aggressor, you have the right to respond in the same manner. This is the standard for self-defense. This verse was revealed in the context of jihad and, as such, its focus is jihad and self-defense. In other words, launching a war is conditional upon enemy aggression. This conditionality of Q. 2:194 is made clear with the particle *man* being followed by *fa*.

Those who believe that offensive jihad is obligatory claim that, "fight the polytheists all together just as they fight you all together" (Q. 9:36), abrogates this verse.[7] In other words, the rule has been abrogated while the verse has been retained as part of the Qurʾan. Evidently, they viewed this injunction as unconditional and absolute. But this position is neither tenable nor acceptable because of the general principle that the unconditional is governed by, and therefore is trumped by, the conditional. Accordingly, the conditional verse, "So if anyone

---

[6] Tabrisi, *Majmaʿ al-bayan*, exegesis of Qurʾan, 2:194.
[7] Muhammad b. Jarir al-Tabari, *Jamiʿ al-bayan ʿan taʾwil ay al-Qurʾan*, exegesis on Qurʾan, 9:36.

commits aggression against you, attack him as he attacked you" (Q. 2:194), trumps the unconditional, "fight the polytheists all together just as they fight you all together" (Q. 9:36). The logical implication of the condition is that initiating an offensive war against the polytheists is unacceptable.

In the words of Muhammad 'Abduh,

> The ruling proclaimed in Q. 2:194, "So if anyone commits aggression against you, attack him as he attacked you," which was revealed in order to make warring against the unbelievers conditional upon them initiating the war, is of a permanent nature and thus was never abrogated. This verse and the previous one are interconnected and related. As such, it is not logical to interject between them a verse from the ninth chapter: "fight the polytheists all together just as they fight you all together" (Q. 9:36). Ibn 'Abbas has related that "this verse has not been abrogated." Accordingly, if anyone considers war as absolute and mandatory even without fulfilling its condition, namely, aggression by the enemy, then this method and style would be alien and constitute a superimposition of one's understanding that is not reconcilable with the verse in question.

> Verses related to war in chapter 3 (*Surah Al 'Imran*) refer to the Battle of Uhud, in which the

unbelievers were the aggressors. Verses related to war in chapter 8 (*Surah al-Anfal*) refer to the Battle of Badr, wherein again the unbelievers were the aggressors and initiators of the war. The verses related to war in chapter 9 (*Surah al-Tawbah*) refer to the polytheists who broke their covenant and started the aggression. Qur'anic verses pertaining to this last group are: "As for those with whom you made a treaty at the Sacred Mosque, so long as they remain true to you, be true to them" (Q. 9:7), and, "How could you not fight a people who have broken their oaths, who tried to drive the Messenger out, who attacked you first?" (Q. 9:13). The polytheists had consistently been at war with the Muslims, fully intending to force them to revert to their earlier belief in polytheism. As such, all the Prophet's wars were in defense and support of the truth. If no one aggresses against the Muslims, compromises their security, or sheds their blood, then God forbids them to fight against others and shed their blood or take their lives. The wars of the Prophet's companions (the first four caliphs) were fought to support the call toward the truth and to end the oppressor's dominance over the Muslims, not for the sake of any material gain. However, wars that occurred under the Umayyads and the Abbasids were launched to establish their dominion by military force.

This is not in harmony with Islam's religious decrees, for it was based on the principle of might makes right.[8]

Qualification of the absolute by the conditional

Up to this point, we have analyzed five Qur'anic verses that mention the condition for engaging in war: the Muslims' right to self-defense against aggressive unbelievers in order to protect themselves from the latter's evil or to aid those who are oppressed. This is in harmony with and is necessitated by human primordial disposition (*fitrah*). These are restrictive verses. In contrast, there are absolute and unconditional verses that order Muslims to fight the unbelievers.

Clearly, these restrictive verses govern and limit the unconditional ones. In reality, conditional verses provide a commentary on the absolute ones and, in the final analysis, govern and restrict the unconditional ones. This general principle is accepted by all conventions and is applicable in all languages.

Second category: Absolute verses

Here we present several Qur'anic verses that are absolute in nature and place no conditions and restrictions on fighting the unbelievers:

---

[8] Rashid Rida, *Tafsir al-Qur'an*, 2:215.

1. "Fighting is ordained for you, though you dislike it. You may dislike something although it is good for you, or like something although it is bad for you: God knows and you do not" (Q. 2:216).

2. "Let those of you who are willing to trade the life of this world for the life to come, fight in God's way. To anyone who fights in God's way, whether killed or victorious, We shall give a great reward" (Q. 4:74).

3. "The believers fight for God's cause, while those who reject faith fight for an unjust cause. Fight the allies of Satan: Satan's ploys are truly weak" (Q. 4:76).

4. "Fight those of the People of the Book who do not [truly] believe in God and the Last Day, who do not forbid what God and His Messenger have forbidden, who do not obey the rule of justice until they pay the tax and agree to submit" (Q. 9:29).

5. "You who believe, fight the disbelievers near you and let them find you standing firm: be aware that God is with those who are mindful of Him" (Q. 9:123).

6. "When you meet the disbelievers in battle, strike them in the neck, and once they are defeated, bind any captives firmly – later you can release them by

grace or by ransom – until the toils of war have ended" (Q. 47:4).

The Prophet's wars were defensive

Based on what has been said above, the Qur'an's verses on jihad clearly permit self-defensive wars only. We know that the first person to apply these verses was the Prophet. From this, we discover that all of his wars were defensive in nature. As a result, Shaykh Muhammad Jawad Balaghi's (d. 1933) assertion is correct:

> All of the Prophet's wars were defensive in nature, for he faced the aggression of oppressive polytheists who sought to annihilate the message of Divine Unity, Shari'ah, and Muslims. He chose the best form of defense that was appropriate in different time periods. Early on, he employed admonition, invited people to reform and peace, and expressed his preference for peace and truce. This was so even when he was victorious, for he would propose an end to violence by signing a peace treaty.[9]

The opinion of Muhammad 'Abduh

Shaykh Muhammad 'Abduh agrees with Shaykh Muhammad Jawad Balaghi. He writes:

---

[9] Muhammad Jawad Balaghi, *al-Rihlah al-madrasiyyah* (Karbala, Mu'assasah al-a'lami, 1963), 212.

Therefore, all of the Prophet's wars were in defense and support of the truth and its people. As a consequence, his invitation (to Islam) before beginning any war was inscribed as a fundamental condition. Obviously, this invitation can take place only with proofs and evidence, not with swords and arrows.[10]

Preservation of peace was the Prophet's practice

Since God commanded the Prophet to struggle to preserve peace, forbade the imposition of Islam by force, and regarded peace as the normative position, it is appropriate to mention one of his actions during the Battle of Badr which exhibits his meticulous adherence to the Qur'anic dictates.

After the Makkan caravan returned safely to Makkah, the advocates of war prepared about one thousand soldiers to annihilate the Muslims and soon established their encampment at a place called Badr. 'Utbah b. Rabi'ah, a prominent Makkan, said to one of his peers while riding on a red-colored camel:

> O people, obey me and do not fight this man and his companions. Bind this affair on my head and blame it on my cowardice. Indeed, among them are men whose relationship is close. The man among you will not stop looking at the killer of his father and his brother. Hatred and malice will be

---

[10] Rashid Rida, *Tafsir al-Qur'an*, 2:215.

bequeathed among you. You will never be able to finish them without them killing the same number among you. Moreover there is no guarantee that you will have success. You seek only the blood of this man and the caravan that was taken. I will carry that and take it upon myself! O people, if Muhammad is false to you, the jackals of the Arabs will take care of him — the jackal of the Arabs is the most destitute of the Arabs; but if he will be your king, you will eat in the kingdom of the son of your brother; and if he will be your prophet you will be the happiest of men with him! O people, do not reject my advice or consider my opinion light witted![11]

The Prophet said about 'Utbah: "If there is a good man in this group he will be the master of that red camel. If they obey him they will be rightly guided."[12]

At this sensitive and delicate juncture, the Prophet acted with brilliance by sending 'Umar b. al-Khattab to the Quraysh with the following message: "Return! I would have preferred it if someone other than you had come to take control of this affair, and I would rather that I take control of the affair from other than you."[13]

---

[11] Abu 'Abdallah Muhammad b. 'Umar al-Waqidi, *Kitab al-maghazi* (*The Life of Muhammad: Al-Waqidi's Kitab al-Maghazi*), trans. Rizwi Faizer, Amal Ismail and AbdulKader Tayob, ed. Rizvi Faizer (New York: Routledge, 2011), 33.
[12] Ibid., 31.
[13] Ibid., 32.

In this proclamation, the Prophet instructs the Makkans to go home and abandon their desire for war. He seeks to exhaust all possible means in order to prevent the onset of war and bloodshed. This is because Qur'an is in accord with human nature, which views peace as normative and foundational and thus condemns offensive war. It therefore commands the Prophet to institute and preserve peace: "But if they incline towards peace, you [Prophet] must also incline towards it, and put your trust in God: He is the All Hearing, the All Knowing" (8:61). By complying with the call of human nature and God's directive, the Prophet shows that his life accords with the Qur'an.

If offensive war for the sake of converting people was allowed, then the Prophet would have instigated hostilities at Badr. The fact that he did not do so is because he was responding in the affirmative to the call of human conscience and God's command. The West, which claims that Islam permits war and bloodshed to forcibly convert people, must pay close attention to this incident, for it reveals the hollowness of their claim.

Peace is the voice of human nature

Goodness, peace, and respectful co-existence are demanded by the human conscience and the Prophet, whose search for peace and opposition to aggressive war is, in actuality, a response to the voice of conscience. The virtues of peace are in such complete accord with human nature that no explanation is necessary. Every person, regardless of his/her faith, unhesitatingly admires those who invite others to peace and seek to draw them away from offensive war. This is why Hakim b. Hizam, the son of Khadijah's brother and the one born inside the Ka'bah[14] (and who eventually became a Muslim) said, upon hearing the Prophet's words: "Muhammad has made a fair and equitable proposal, and it is obligatory [upon us] to accept it. I swear by God that if you still insist on going to war after he has made this equitable proposal, then you will not attain victory over him."[15] So deeply anchored is the love and affinity for peace in human nature that even a Makkan unbeliever tried to discourage his people from going to war by predicting their defeat. History records that he was right.

Critical scholarly opinions based on evidentiary proofs from the Qur'an and the Prophet's conduct (*sirah*)

The Qur'an and the Prophet's practices categorically prohibit launching a war to convert unbelievers. However, with great surprise and astonishment we see that jurists, when discussing jihad in their jurisprudential works, regard the foundational jihad as consisting of initiating an offensive war for that very purpose.

We will bring forth a few examples of this below.

---

[14]Nasrallah b. Muhammad b. al-Athir, *Asad al-ghabah fi ma'rifah al-sahabah* (Cairo: al-Matba'ah al-wahbiyyah, 1864), 2:40.

[15] Waqidi, *Kitab al-Maghazi*, 1:61.

Imam Shafi'i (d. 820)

In his *Umm*, imam Shafi'i says:

> God blessed a group of people to embrace Islam
> and become Companions after the Prophet
> migrated to Madinah. With divine help, their
> numbers grew to a level that was unparalleled.
> Thus, God made jihad obligatory upon them even
> though it had not been so in the past: "Fighting is
> ordained for you, though you dislike it. You may
> dislike something although it is good for you, or
> like something although it is bad for you: God
> knows and you do not" (Q. 2:216); "Fight in
> God's cause against those who fight you, but do
> not overstep the limits: God does not love those
> who overstep the limits" (Q. 2:190); "Strive hard
> for God as is His due" (Q. 22:78); "When you
> meet the disbelievers in battle, strike them in the
> neck, and once they are defeated, bind any
> captives firmly – later you can release them by
> grace or by ransom – until the toils of war have
> ended" (Q. 47:4); and "If you do not go out and
> fight, God will punish you severely and put others
> in your place, but you cannot harm Him in any
> way: God has power over all things" (Q. 9:39).[16]

---

[16] Muhammd b. Idris al-Shafi'i, *Kitab al-umm*, ed. M. Zahir al-Najjar
(Beirut: Dar al-ma'rifah, n.d.), 4:161.

Here, basing himself upon these Qur'anic verses, he rules that initiating offensive wars against the unbelievers is just as obligatory as are the obligatory prayers and fasting. But by citing only those verses that have an absolute (*mutlaqah*) nature, he has deliberately left out the particularized or restrictive verses which make war conditional upon enemy aggression. He did this not because he is unaware of them, but because he considers all of them to have been abrogated. Before he starts his discussion on the absolute verses, he states:

God has said that those who are the victims of oppression and have been expelled from their homeland are permitted to engage in jihad, as recorded in the following verses: "Those who have been attacked are permitted to take up arms because they have been wronged – God has the power to help them – those who have been driven unjustly from their homes only for saying, 'Our Lord is God'" (Q. 22:39); "Fight in God's cause against those who fight you, but do not overstep the limits: God does not love those who overstep the limits" (Q. 2:190); and "Do not fight them at the Sacred Mosque unless they fight you there. If they do fight you, kill them" (Q. 2:191). All of the verses that made fighting the unbelievers conditional upon the latter initiating the attack were abrogated by Q. 2:193: "Fight them until there is no more persecution [*fitnah*], and [your] worship is devoted to God." This verse was revealed after the obligation of jihad had been instituted.[17]

---

[17] Ibid.

Other jurists and Qur'anic exegetes before him, among them 'Abd al-Rahman b. Zayd b. Aslam and Rabi'ah b. Anas, make the same claim.[18] Shafi'i relates the opinion of such scholars, but does not mention their names.

But what, it must be asked, was the rationale for ignoring the accepted principle that absolute verses must be read in the context of particularized verses, a matter that is so clear on the basis of convention and commentary on the principles? All experts in the field have subscribed to it at all times and places and have acted upon it, and will continue to do so in the future. So why was this timeless principle not applied in the case of verses dealing with jihad?

In the final analysis, Islam's global image was tarnished and polluted; the rule of human nature on self-defense established by the particularized verses became distorted; and, in its place, launching an offensive war to impose Islam was introduced as the essence of jihad. Did politics influence this outcome? Were such people as Rabi' b. Anas and 'Abd al-Rahman b. Zayd b. Aslam influenced by the caliph, under whose rule offensive wars were initiated and the blood of those who sought peace was shed in order to expand the empire's territorial domain?

Obviously, in such a stifling political environment, no one would have the courage to issue a legal ruling against offensive war, or to interpret Qur'anic verses in any way

---

[18] Tabrisi, *Majma' al-bayan*, exegesis on Qur'an, 2:190.

which would indict the oppressive ruler for such an injustice. Likewise, Muhammad 'Abduh has said that these wars were motivated by the impulse of forcible territorial expansion and the subsequent invasion of its own neighbors. All of this violated the Islamic dictates.[19]

Here we will cite a few examples to provide a glimpse of the crimes committed in the name of jihad and also of that time's political climate.

During the Umayyad period (661-750), Hajjaj b. Yusuf Thaqafi appointed Qutayba b. Muslim Bahili governor of Khurasan. This man attacked its capital city, Bukhara, and due to his military prowess was able to conquer it. He then marched on to Taliqan, which was under Bazam's control and dominance. Qutayba, fully aware of the fact that Bazam's son was accompanying him, exploited the situation by summoning and then hanging the son along with others. After this, he fought with Bazam for a few days, overpowered him, and executed both him and his family. After this, a Muslim convert named 'Abdallah (formerly known as Neyzak-e Tarkhun), petitioned Qutayba for permission to move back to his native place of Takharistan. Upon arriving, he enlisted a large number of non-Arabs into the army. When Qutayba launched an offensive war against Takharistan, he sent Salim Nasih, one of 'Abdallah's friends and confidants, to talk with him. His actual intent, however, was to deceive 'Abdallah. Salim, on Qutayba's behalf, assured 'Abdallah

---

[19] Rashid Rida, *Tafsir al-Qur'an*, 2:216.

that all of demands, without exception, would be accepted. Finally, he personally assured 'Abdallah that his own safety was guaranteed before sending him to Qutayba. But Qutayba, ignoring the agreement Salim had devised in his name, killed 'Abdallah and his nephew and sent their heads to Hajjaj. Moreover, he intended to rape his wife. When he was alone with her, she said: "How ignorant you are. Did you think that by killing my husband and conquering our country would make me subservient to you?!" Qutayba freed her and said: "Go to wherever you please."[20]

In such a dictatorial and suffocating atmosphere, pious jurists and Qur'anic exegetes had to adopt dissimulation (*taqiyyah*) to survive, and were forced to conduct themselves in ways designed to prevent a direct confrontation with the ruler. Those with lower degrees of piety, most likely, would be inclined to express their support for the rulers.

In any event, the claim that the particularistic verses on jihad have been abrogated and that aggressive jihad is therefore obligatory, were used to justify the conduct of oppressive rulers. The fact that their behavior did not agree with that of the Prophet was ignored. This view was accepted by a number of exegetes and jurists who were qualified to issue legal opinions; it was still being followed at the time of imam Shafi'i. He accepted this

---

[20] Ahmad al-Ya'qubi, *Ta'rikh al-Ya'qubi* (Najaf: Matba'ah al-ghurri, 1939-40), 3:31 and 32.

view and, basing himself upon it, issued a *fatwa* (legal ruling) [that offensive war is obligatory]. We do not know whether he issued it willingly or under duress and necessity. But we do know this much: During his lifetime, this view was established and not open to refutation, and thus he fell under its influence. Naturally, one can expect that this established precedent had a strong impact upon the decision-making process and rulings of both contemporaneous and subsequent Sunni and Shi'i jurists. All of them ruled that to launch an offensive war to invite unbelievers to Islam or, more accurately, to impose Islam upon them through military force, is permissible.

We now provide examples of statements made by various jurists.

Ibn Humam Hanafi (d. 1457)

Ibn Humam Hanafi says in *Fath al-Qadir*:

> Fighting against unbelievers is obligatory even if they are not the aggressors and initiators of war, because the proofs and evidence that make offensive war obligatory have not made war conditional upon their initiation of the war. In addition, the prophetic hadith in *Sahih Bukhari*, *Sahih Muslim*, and other books explicitly state: 'I am ordered to fight people until they say there is no god but Allah.' This hadith, without any

hesitation, is a proof that it is obligatory for Muslims to initiate war against the unbelievers.[21]

His claim that "the proofs and evidence that make offensive war obligatory have not made war conditional upon their initiation of the war," can be refuted in the following manner:

The most authoritative proofs, those Qur'anic verses related to jihad, are of two types: absolute and restrictive. The restrictive verses condition the obligation of offensive jihad upon the unbelievers' initiation of aggression against the Muslims. Thus, the absolute verses have to be circumscribed by the conditional verses. For example, someone tells you to "host the religious scholars" but "do not host non-Hashimi religious scholars." If you then invite non-Hashimi instead of Hashimi religious scholars, you cannot argue that "I acted on the basis of the absolute command to invite the religious scholars." Due to the presence of the directive, "Do not invite non-Hashimi religious scholars," the absoluteness is no longer operative because it is now governed by the restrictive sentence. Clearly, Ibn Humam did not act on the basis of the particularistic verses on jihad, but on the absolute verses.

There are two possibilities here: (1) he was unaware of the principle that the absolute is circumscribed by the particular, which is almost impossible to surmise for a

---

[21] Muhammad b. Humam Hanafi, *Sharh Fath al-qadir* (Cairo: Mustafa al-Babi al-Halabi, 1970), 5:194.

learned jurist, or (2) he could not dissociate himself from his time's established view and so, just like Shafi'i did, issued a *fatwa* under its influence: "Particularistic verses on jihad have been abrogated and cannot be advanced as proof." This claim is baseless and unacceptable. In fact, it differs markedly from logic employed by Tabari, a prominent exegete, in his commentary on 2:190: "Fight in God's cause against those who fight you, but do not overstep the limits: God does not love those who overstep the limits": "The claim that this verse has been abrogated is an instance of a legal ruling that is oppressive and unreasonable because there is no proof at all to support it."[22] Tabari's position is correct, and to believe otherwise is so incredulous that every independent jurist should definitely seek to avoid doing so.

And then there is the prophetic hadith upon which Ibn Humam depends for his conclusion: "I am ordered to fight people until they say there is no god but Allah." It is necessary to point out here that even if we accept this hadith as a valid proof, its application should be circumscribed based on the principle that absolute verses are governed by restrictive verses. As such, it could be interpreted as: "I am given a mandate to fight against the aggressors for as long as they remain unbelievers and persist in their aggression. But, if they embrace Islam by reciting the *shahadah*, then naturally they would stop their aggression and this would bring an end to the conflict."

---

[22] Tabari, *Jami' al-bayan*, exegesis on 2:190.

Just as a legal manual is viewed as an interrelated integral and cohesive entity, such that its absolute aspects are governed by its particularistic ones, likewise those Qur'anic verses which are linked with reliable hadiths should be viewed in the same way. This naturally lends itself to the principle that absolute verses are circumscribed by the particularistic ones. In the final analysis, therefore, one cannot act upon the absolute nature of the verse or of the hadith. As such, if the afore-mentioned hadith were to be interpreted in conjunction with the restrictive verses, it would produce the same interpretation that we have posited. Ibn Humam has latched onto the absolute signification of this specific hadith without paying attention to the particularistic verses. He has followed this same unscholarly and unacceptable method when elucidating the Qur'anic verses pertaining to jihad.

Shaykh Tusi (d. 1067)

Intellectual and cultural exchange has been a common occurrence among Sunni and Shi'i scholars. Shaykh Tusi's approach, formulated while living and conducting research in Baghdad, was to consult the Sunni sources and retrieve a selection of material for use in his analysis of Islamic law, Qur'anic exegesis, and other disciplines. One who examines his *tafsir, al-Tibyan*, would no doubt observe that he relied upon those of Tabari, Rammani, and other Sunni exegetes and followed their method of exegesis. Likewise, in the discipline of *fiqh*, he consulted the works of Sunni scholars. *Mabsut*, his most exhaustive *fiqh* work, is written using the *ijtihadi* (scholarly) approach of Sunni scholars. Thus, one would expect him to fall under the influence of that particular times' dominant approach and ideas when deducing legal verdicts and, subsequently, to validate the legal rulings of his Sunni peers. These rulings would then find their way into books, including Shaykh Tusi's, which deal with *fiqh*. Such an expectation is completely justified in his case and in the cases of all other jurists living at a time when Sunni *fiqh* dominated the intellectual circles. Thus, Shaykh Tusi holds the same position as did imam Shafi'i, which is laid out in his *fiqh* books without any critical analysis. In his book of legal rulings, *al-Nihaya*, he writes:

> Those who must be fought against and challenged are as follows: The first groups are those who must be given the choice either to accept Islam or be fought against. They may be taken as slaves and their assets are confiscated as spoils of war. They include all different groups of non-believers, but not Jews, Christians or Magians/Zoroastrians. These last three groups are regarded as the people of the book (*ahl al-kitab* or the people of scripture). The second group are those who would pay *jizyah* (a head tax paid by the people who would not accept Islam but would accept being under the protection of Muslims). They are the Jews, the Christians and the Zoroastrians. They are protected, not killed and not taken as slaves provided they pay the poll tax and abide by the conditions (*dhimmah*) of *jizyah*. They will be

treated like others if they refuse to pay *jizyah* or interfere with and/or disregard the terms and conditions of their treaty. In this case they, are fought against, taken captive as slaves and their properties are taken as spoils of war.

It is not allowed to fight any non-believer unless they are invited to Islam first, and before being asked to declare their submission to Allah, their acceptance of the divine mission of Muhammad, their belief in monotheism, the justice of Allah and their agreement to behave according to the Islamic code of practice (*shari'ah*). Once they are given the choice and they refuse it, then it is obligatory to fight them. It is not allowed to kill them if they have not been presented with the choice of accepting Islam. The choice should be presented by the Imam himself or by his deputy. It is not allowed to fight and kill women. If they fight Muslims and help their husbands and men who are fighting Muslims and have entered into war against Muslims, then they should be only prevented or arrested. If the Muslims are forced by circumstances to fight them (the women) then it is allowed to do so; there is nothing wrong with this.

The main condition and term of *dhimmah* (protection of the non-Muslim subjects of the Muslim state by Muslims) is (to fully accept the authority of Muslim state and) not openly challenge the Muslim community, for example by consuming pork, drinking alcoholic beverages, taking interest, and marrying those whom one is not allowed to marry according to Islamic law. If they ignore any of these rules, they have ignored the terms of *dhimmah* and must be treated as unbelievers. He who has converted to Islam but still lives in the enemy territory (*dar al-harb*) should not be killed and his young children (*sighar*) should also be treated as Muslims. The grown-up members of his family and those who refuse Islam are treated as non-believers.[23]

One notices the extent to which the dominant intellectual discourse influenced him and how he could not insulate himself from it. As a result, he gave the same legal ruling as did Shafi'i and considered it to be the most acceptable opinion.

We are confident that if Shaykh Tusi had remained outside the orbit of Sunni influence and examined the verses on jihad, he would have concluded that the restrictive verses on jihad both trump and confine the absolute verses. In other words, he would have concluded that offensive war is permissible only when the enemy initiates it against the Muslims. War is, by its very nature, something detested and unpleasant; however, rational and religious bases do provide a justification for self-defense. This is exactly what jihad is. But the shaykh, surrounded

---

[23] Muhammad b. Hasan al-Tusi, *al-Nihayah fi mujarrad al-fiqh wa al-fatawa* (*Al-Nihayah: A Concise Description of Islamic Law and Legal Opinions*), trans. A. Ezzati (London: ICAS, 2008), 216-17.

by the predominant Sunni religious discourse, could not see this.

Thus we can neither emulate his *fatwa* nor accept his *ijtihad* on this matter. All we can do is criticize it, just as we did the *fatwa* of imam Shafi'i.

Ibn Idris (d. 1202)

Ibn Idris al-Hilli writes in his *Sara'ir*:

> Warring against the unbelievers is not permissible without first inviting them to Islam, which entails their acceptance of the dual testimony of faith, confirmation of their belief in oneness of God (*tawhid*), justice, and all the rules pertaining to Islam. After they have been invited to Islam in this format and if they still refuse to accept it, then it is allowed to go to war against them.[24]

He opines that unbelievers should be invited to Islam via military force, for their refusal to convert justifies the launch of an offensive war which can be pursued until they either accept Islam or are killed. Evidently, the scholar either ignored the conditional verses on jihad or considered them to have been abrogated. From this perspective, he considered offensive war against unbelievers obligatory if they refused to convert. In

---

[24] Ibn Idris al-Hilli, *al-Sara'ir* (Qum: Mu'assasah al-nashr al-Islami al-tabi'ah li jama'ah al-mudarrisin, 1990), 2:6.

actuality, he accepted the *fatwa* of Shaykh Tusi, who, in turn, had embraced the *fatwa* of Shafi'i.

I would like to make a point here. The verse, "So if they withdraw and do not fight you, and offer you peace, then God gives you no way against them" (Q. 4:90), clearly prohibits initiating war against any unbelievers who are seeking peace or a truce with the Muslims. This is only one of the conditional verses not brought forth in the earlier discourse. In any event, according to this verse and the others mentioned above, offensive war against this category of unbelievers is not allowed under any circumstance.

In contrast, the verse following it obliges Muslims to defend themselves against aggressive unbelievers who initiate war: "So if they neither withdraw, nor offer you peace, nor restrain themselves from fighting you, seize and kill them wherever you encounter them. We give you clear authority against such people" (Q. 4:91).

'Allamah Hilli (d. 1325)

'Allamah Hilli writes in his *Tadhkirah*:

> It is obligatory upon Muslims to set off for war against those with whom it is mandated to go to war, whether it be in a form of pre-emptive strike or for the sake of converting them to Islam. Those who are sought after to convert must first be invited to Islam and to accept its precepts. In the

event that they accept these terms, they are free to go. But if they reject them, then it is mandatory to initiate war against them.[25]

Thus 'Allamah Hilli, just like Shaykh Tusi and Ibn Idris, also ignored the crucial point: Conditional verses on jihad that allow fighting the unbelievers are contingent upon the latter's aggression. If he had paid attention to this fact, he would not have issued such a *fatwa*. In any event, our objections to his position are the same as those that we have leveled against imam Shafi'i, Shaykh Tusi, and Ibn Idris.

Shahid II (Zayn al-Din al-'Amili) (d. 1558)

In *Sharh lum'ah,* Shahid II says: "Jihad is of different types: one is offensive war against the unbelievers in order to invite them to Islam; [the] other is jihad against those unbelievers who aggress upon the Muslims."[26]

My rebuttal of this opinion is the same as the one I put forth in the case of Tusi, Ibn Idris and 'Allamah Hilli: If Shahid II had paid attention to the restrictive Qur'anic verses, then he would not have issued a legal opinion allowing Muslims to fight unbelievers in order to convert them. In any event, these legal rulings are baseless and

---

[25] Hasan b. Yusuf al-Hilli, *Tadhkirah al-fuqaha'* (Qum: al-Maktabah al-murtadawiyyah li ihya' al-turath al-athar al-Ja'fariyyah, 1968), 1:409.

[26] Zay al-Din al-'Amili (Shahid II), *Sharh al-lum'ah* (Qum: Intisharat-e dawari, 1989), 2:379.

cannot be sustained for they lack any reliable proof and contradict the restrictive jihad verses.

Muhammad Hasan al-Najafi (Sahib Jawahir) (d. 1849)

Shaykh Najafi writes:

> There is no doubt that the foundational jihad is the same as offensive war against the unbelievers in order to invite them to accept Islam. The verse that says: 'Fighting is ordained for you, though you dislike it. You may dislike something although it is good for you, or like something although it is bad for you' (Q. 2:216) was revealed in connection with offensive war.[27]

Najafi makes two claims here: (1) the primary jihad is launching an offensive war to convert unbelievers and (2) that Q. 2:216 was revealed in connection with just such an undertaking. Regarding his first claim, we say that, based on our earlier discourse, those conditional verses dealing with jihad trump the absolute verses and, as such, the primary jihad consists of fighting the unbelievers *only if they initiate the hostilities*. In other words, the primary jihad is self-defense.

With regards to his second claim, the verse following the one he cited says: "They will not stop fighting you [believers] until they make you revoke your faith, if they

---

[27] Muhammad Hasan al-Najafi, *Jawahir al-kalam* (Qum: Dar al-kutub al-Islamiyyah, 1983), 21:4.

can" (Q. 2:217). In accordance with this verse, Q. 2:216 was clearly revealed in response to the unbelievers' persistent attacks. It therefore refutes Najafi's contention that Q. 2:216 was revealed to permit Muslims to engage in an offensive war against unbelievers. Rather, it was revealed within the context of the unbelievers' launching of military attacks to force the Muslims to revert to their earlier religion. The commentary on the afore-mentioned verse, within the context of the following verse, is: "Defensive war, in response to the unbelievers' military offensive, is obligatory even though this option does not appeal to you as it entails hardship and incurs loss. In actuality, however, it is to your benefit because through it you are repelling the evil and harm of the aggressive enemies. It may be to your liking not to enter into a defensive war, whereas not doing so in actuality will be to your disadvantage and loss in the long run. Ultimately, regaining a state of peace and repose will demand even greater hardship and difficulty for you."

Invitation to religion by military force?

In the writings of Ibn Idris, 'Allamah Hilli, Shahid II, and Shaykh Najafi, we observe that initiating offensive war against unbelievers to convert them has been made obligatory. In reality, such an interpretation is no more than demanding the imposition of Islam by military force. It is important to note that their statements are diametrically opposed to the Qur'anic verses that declare: "[O Prophet], call people to the way of your Lord with wisdom and beautiful teaching. Argue with them in the

most courteous way" (Q. 16:125); "there is no compulsion
in religion" (Q. 2:256); "We guided him to the right path,
whether he was grateful or not" (Q. 76:3); and, "Say,
'Now the truth has come from your Lord: let those who
wish to believe in it do so, and let those who wish to
reject it do so" (Q. 18:29).

In essence, the act of inviting others to the path of truth is
associated with logic, proofs, advice, and the seeking out
of others' welfare, none of which are compatible with
threats and force. Imposing Islam by military means can
never be considered a true invitation, for how can one
make a free choice in an atmosphere of intimidation and
fear of death? As such, labeling it as an "invitation" is
either a joke or a meaningless metaphor. In any event, the
jurists' assertion that jihad means imposing Islam by
military force in the form of an invitation is incompatible
with both explicit Qur'anic verses, and intellect, and
human nature (*fitrah*). Therefore, it cannot be accepted. In
fact, this opinion ought to be judged as both illogical and
unacceptable. Moreover, the Qur'anic ethos distances and
dissociates itself from such a position. No jurist should
claim that, "fighting is ordained for you, though you
dislike it" (Q. 2:216) was revealed to institute offensive
war against unbelievers.

Acceptable invitation under the rubric of jihad

Some hadiths mention inviting unbelievers to Islam
before initiating a war, like the one related on the
authority of Imam 'Ali: "When the Prophet sent me to

Yemen he said: 'O 'Ali, do not fight with anyone before first inviting him to Islam. I swear by God that if He guides even one person through you, it is better for you than possessing the area on which the sun rises and sets.'"[28]

In the hadith related by Buraydah, the Prophet states that whenever he appointed a commander over his forces, he advised them as follows: "Whenever you have a confrontation with the polytheistic enemies, invite them to accept one of these three things. Whichever one that they accept, consent to it and let them go free. The first one is to invite them to Islam. If they accept it, then you should stop fighting against them..."[29]

Keeping in mind that the Qur'an prohibits offensive war against the unbelievers, it would be natural to expect that these two hadiths would be analyzed in the context of aggression committed by unbelievers. As we explained earlier, repelling the evil of attacking unbelievers can be achieved by other and far more preferable methods. One of them is to invite them to Islam via admonition and guidance. In fact, this is regarded as the topmost and primary responsibility of the Prophet and all other messengers. Under this scenario and condition, the confrontation would end when the aggressive unbelievers

---

[28] Al-Hurr al-'Amili, *Wasa'il al-Shi'ah*, ed. Muhammad al-Razi (Beirut: Dar ihya al-turath al-'Arabi, 1983), 11:30, hadith no. 1.
[29] Majd al-Din al-Mubarak Ibn Athir, *Jami' al-usul fi ahadith al-Rasul* (Beirut: Dar Ibn Athir, 1991-), 3:201.

convert and both parties are reconciled. From this point on, they would be regarded as fellow Muslims.

This kind of invitation, which is both logical and pleasant, is one way to secure peace and remove the prospect of war. It reminds one of 'Ali's invitation to Amr b. 'Abdawud during the Battle of the Ditch: "I offer you three options, the first one of which is acceptance of Islam."[30] If Amr had accepted Islam, his status within the enemy camp would have brought about a major transformation in the unbelievers' psyche. His conversion could have ended the aggression and become a basis for peace.

This kind of invitation, in contrast to the supposed "primary jihad" mentioned above, is fundamentally different for its sole intention is to do good and guide the attacking unbelievers. In such a situation, the Muslim commander would say to his unbelieving counterpart: "If you accept Islam voluntarily, then you will attain guidance and prevent bloodshed." But according to the jurists cited above, Muslims can attack even those unbelievers who intend no harm to the Muslims and who are at peace with them on the pretext of inviting them to Islam. Such an approach does not constitute guidance; in reality, it is nothing but coercion and imposition, both of which are fundamentally incompatible with the Islamic ethos.

---

[30] Waqidi, *Kitab al-Maghazi*, 1:471.

'Ali went to Yemen to guide the people

It is important to note that 'Ali's trip to Yemen, which was mentioned in connection with the first hadith, was for the sake of guidance and not for war. His predecessor, Khalid b. Walid, had been commissioned to guide the Yemenis; six months later, there were still no converts. So the Prophet replaced him with 'Ali. Khalid, along with the forces accompanying him (except Bara' b. 'Azib) returned, and the latter is reported to have said:

> We were in 'Ali's army. When we got close to Yemenis, they received this news and prepared for war. 'Ali led the morning prayers and he lined us up in rows. He stood in front of us and the Yemenis. After praising and glorifying God, he read out the Prophet's letter. As a result of its oratory and depth, all of them converted to Islam on the same day. 'Ali conveyed this news to the Prophet, who became happy and performed a prostration of thanks.[31]

Although 'Ali's mission was to guide the Yemenis, he was accompanied by a contingent of soldiers as a mark of caution. The Prophet, before sending him, said: "Do not war against anyone without first inviting him/her to Islam," which is interpreted to mean that "if you encounter aggression while on this mission of guidance,

---

[31] Abu Abdullah Muhammad al-Harithi (Shaykh Mufid), *Kitab al-irshad* (*The Book of Guidance*), trans. I. K. A. Howard (London: Muhammadi Trust, 1981), 39.

invite them to Islam before responding to them militarily." It has been substantiated that 'Ali did not initiate the battles of the Camel, Siffin, and Nahrawan; rather, they were imposed upon him by the transgressors.

Proofs advanced by 'Allamah Tabataba'i (d. 1981)

We have shown above that the early jurists regarded the primary jihad as launching an offensive war to impose Islam by military force. As far as we know, this position was adopted into the codified *fiqh* during the time of imam Shafi'i and subsequently accepted as the norm, for subsequent jurists presented it without the slightest hesitation as a legal ruling beyond contestation and dissent. The author of *al-Mizan* also accepted its legitimacy, and viewed it as both natural and logical:

> The Qur'an says that Islam and the religion of the *tawhid* (monotheism) of God is based on the foundation of human nature and its mandate is to reform human beings because God has said: "So [Prophet] as a man of pure faith, stand firm in your devotion to the religion. This is the natural disposition God instilled in mankind – there is no altering God's creation – and this is the right religion, though most people do not realize it" (Q. 30:30). Accordingly, establishing and preserving Islam and the religion of *tawhid* is a human being's most important right, and its defense is also vital based on human nature. God has said in this regard: "If God did not repel some people by

means of others, many monasteries, churches, synagogues, and mosques, where God's name is much invoked, would have been destroyed" (Q. 22:40) and "O believers, respond to God and His Messenger when he calls you to that which gives you life" (Q. 8:24). Jihad is something that enlivens humanity and therefore war – whether it be for defense of the Muslims, or one of their important sites, or an offensive war against the unbelievers – all of them, in actuality, are in defense of the right of human beings. Jihad should perpetually remain operative because polytheism is a cause for humanity's destruction and the death of human nature (*fitrah*). War and jihad are a source of giving life to humanity after its death. Thus, the war mentioned in the Qur'an is either for annihilating polytheism or making the word of truth supreme over the People of the Book in order to force them into paying the poll tax (*jizyah*). The objection that war is invoked to coerce people to accept Islam is not sustainable, because giving life to humanity is conditional upon imposing the truth on a group of people after having presented them with demonstrative proofs. This is analogous to something that is common in all nation states: if someone violates a country's civil statutes, then first he/she would be instructed to follow the rules, failing which the law is imposed without any discrimination. Moreover, force and the imposition of Islam is limited to the first generation only, because subsequent generations, due to proper religious upbringing, will accept the religion of human nature by their own free will and choice.[32]

It is necessary to point out a few matters here.

1. As Islam prohibits the launching of an offensive jihad to impose Islam through military force, it is pointless to enter into any discussion designed to rationalize it. In other words, it is a waste of time to fabricate justifications for any interpretation that contradicts the human intellect and the Qur'an.

2. Just as each person has the right to accept *tawhid*, each person also has the inalienable right to reject it. Islam never removes this right when it comes to the matter of religion: "There is no compulsion in religion: true guidance has become distinct from error" (Q. 2:256); "Say, 'Now the truth has come from your Lord: let those who wish to believe in it do so, and let those who wish to reject it do so" (Q. 18:29); and, "We guided him to the right path, whether he was grateful or not" (Q. 76:3). These verses were never abrogated. In fact, they will continue to proclaim until the Day of Judgment that people are free to choose which religion they

---

[32] Muhammad Husayn al-Tabataba'i, *al-Mizan fi tafsir al-Qur'an* (Qum: Mu'assasah al-nashr al-Islami al-tabi'ah li jama'ah al-mudarrisin, 1981), 2:66-67.

will follow. It is neither rational nor just to remove one right (i.e. freedom in the choice of belief and religion) to protect another right, primordial religion of monotheism (*tawhid-e fitri*).

3. The statement that one aspect of war and jihad is to annihilate polytheism contradicts reality, because jihad is a natural reaction to the oppression perpetrated by one's enemies: "Those who have been attacked are permitted to take up arms because they have been wronged" (Q. 22:39). If offensive jihad to destroy polytheism was obligatory, then the Prophet would not have accepted any truce with the polytheists at Hudaybiyyah; rather, he would have fought them to impose Islam on them. In addition, he would not have allowed the Makkan polytheists, after their city fell, to remain loyal to their polytheistic beliefs. Nor would he have entered into a reciprocal agreement with the polytheists of the Khuza'i tribe, one that required the Muslims to defend these polytheists if they were attacked. If the assertion presented above is true, the Prophet would have initiated an offensive war in each instance both to suppress them and to impose Islam. Over and beyond all of this, in essence, polytheism is a matter of belief that resides in the heart. Thus, it cannot be destroyed by war and weapons, because weapons are effective only on one's body.

4. Yet another claim, that another type of jihad
    consists of fighting the People of the Book to
    bring about the supremacy of truth over their
    belief system in order to humble them into
    accepting payment of poll tax (*jizyah*), can be
    refuted. Its adherents cite: "Fight those of the
    People of the Book who do not [truly] believe in
    God and the Last Day, who do not forbid what
    God and His Messenger have forbidden, who do
    not obey the rule of justice until they pay the tax
    and agree to submit" (Q. 9:29). This verse is one
    of the absolute verses and, in accordance with the
    known rules mentioned earlier, it therefore must
    be circumscribed by the particularistic verses on
    jihad. As such, the meaning of this verse would
    become: "Fight against those members of the
    People of the Book who have attacked you. When
    the fighting ends and they have been humbled,
    obtain their agreement to pay the poll tax." As
    such, the aforementioned verse does not intend to
    convey the sense that it is mandatory to initiate
    such a war.

5. His analogy between imposing Islam by force and
    enforcing civil statutes on the one guilty of
    violating them is deficient, because such
    enforcement pertains to one who has agreed to
    abide by the system that established the rules. Any
    violation of it, therefore, would naturally entail
    some form of punishment. This is not the case
    with launching an offensive war against

unbelievers, because they have not accepted Islam. In addition, implementing civil law by force does not involve imposing Islam; rather, it consists of the just enforcement of laws upon those who voluntarily accepted to abide by the system which laid out the rules. If one who has voluntarily accepted this system subsequently violates it, punishment is justified.

6. As for their statement that "polytheism is a cause of destruction of humanity and the death of human nature (*fitrah*)," is this state restricted to those who are guilty of polytheism or of destroying humanity as a whole or human nature (*fitrah*) on a universal level? Obviously, the presence of a number of polytheists does not result in such a situation, for the adverse effects are confined to this group alone. Thus, their own belief system causes their misfortune. One cannot say, for instance, that the polytheistic practices of a few Makkans could bring about the total and complete destruction of humanity in all places which can be revived only by the initiation of offensive war against the polytheists. As a result, the general statement about polytheism, along with its supposed "universality," is not in harmony with reality. Rather, polytheism is the cause of destruction of humanity in the person himself/herself who subscribes to this belief system because he/she has voluntarily chosen falsehood.

7. If launching an offensive war against unbelievers to impose Islam was obligatory and constituted the primary and foundational form of jihad, as 'Allamah Tabataba'i and others maintain, then the Prophet himself would have done so. The best and most opportune time to have done this would have been during the conquest of Makkah, when he enjoyed enormous power. But instead of forcing the Makkans to choose between Islam and the sword, he announced that anyone who stayed within the confines of his/her house or in Abu Sufyan's house, as well as in a mosque, would be safe.[33]

This amnesty and security was granted only to unbelievers, for those who were already Muslim did not need any form of security. The Prophet asked the Makkans: "'O Quraysh, what do you think that I am about to do with you?' They replied, 'Good. You are a noble brother, son of a noble brother.' He said, "Go your way for you are the freed ones (*tulaqa'*).'"[34] It would have been redundant to tell the Muslims that they are free and secure, so he could only have been telling the unbelievers to remain faithful to their own belief system. Accordingly, he did not impose Islam on them by military force under the slogan of jihad.

---

[33] 'Abd al-Malik b. Hisham, *The Life of Muhammad: A Translation of Ishaq's Sirat Rasul Allah*, trans. Alfred Guillaume (New York: Oxford University Press, 1955), 548.
[34] Ibid., 553.

What is the response of the jurists?

It has become evident from our past discussion that from the time of imam Shafi'i onward, the jurists ignored the conditional verses on jihad that had made fighting the unbelievers dependent on the latter's initiation of the war. Instead, they considered the primary jihad to be offensive warfare against the unbelievers for the sake of imposing Islam. In order to appreciate the essence of such thinking and its adverse effects, we will provide the following hypothetical scenario:

Suppose that a military contingent is prepared to implement the jurists' offensive war *fatwa* against countries inhabited by non-hostile unbelievers who desire peace and a harmonious coexistence with the Muslims. But as a precaution, they have prepared a military force and are, along with the Muslims, ready to fight. Before any belligerent act, the Muslim commander approaches and says: "We invite you to embrace Islam, otherwise war will be declared upon you." The unbelievers' representative could reply: "But your scripture proclaims: '[O Prophet], call people to the way of your Lord with wisdom and beautiful teaching. Argue with them in the most courteous way' (Q. 16:25). Now, instead of following this directive and presenting us with sound arguments and proofs, you threaten us with military force. What kind of invitation is this that employs military force? Such intimidation neither makes our hearts incline toward Islam nor prepares them to embrace it. Rather, it has a negative effect and makes us become stubborn and intransigent. You should not label your approach as an *invitation,* because it is no more than an ultimatum for combat directed against a non-hostile people who harbor no ill-will toward you, a people who only want to live in peace and harmony with you. We aspire for this, and find war and the shedding of blood repulsive."

The Muslim commander could reply by saying: "We are people of combat and, based on our jurists' *fatwas*, must engage in offensive war, as this is the primary form of jihad in Islam." The unbelievers could remonstrate: "Even though your Qur'an states: 'But if they incline toward peace, you [O Prophet] must also incline toward it and put your trust in God' (Q. 8:61)? This calls for peace, and yet you call for war. We want to live in peace and with mutual respect. Why are you acting contrary to your own holy book? Why do you want to attack a non-hostile people who seek peace?" They would reply: "Our hearts are full of hatred and spite against you, for believers are supposed to be 'harsh toward the disbelievers and compassionate toward each other'" (Q. 48:29). And the reply would be: "This sternness and hatred is with regards to those unbelievers who are attacking the Muslims, not those who are not attacking them. Your Qur'an states: 'And He does not forbid you to deal kindly and justly with anyone who has not fought you for your faith or driven you out of your homes: God loves the just' (Q. 60:8). The implied meaning here is that you are admonished to do good concerning those who are not hostile to you and to deal with them in fairness and equity. Do you think that it is a mark of righteousness and justice to start an offensive war against us, as well as to kill us and orphan our children, even though we have no ill will against you?"

The Muslim commander would reply: "According to the jurists, the primary form of jihad is offensive war against the unbelievers for the sake of imposing Islam. This entitles one to great reward, and we are required to do this." We would hear a response: "But your Qur'an proclaims: 'There is no compulsion in religion: true guidance has become distinct from error' (Q. 2:256). How do you intend to impose Islam, contrary to the Qur'an's directives, by force and military might?" They would reply: "Do not dialogue with us by invoking the Qur'an, because we do not understand it and our obligation is to follow the jurists' *fatwas*, for only they understand it. They have instructed us to engage in offensive war against the unbelievers until they forcibly accept Islam." The response would be: "You seem to only rely upon their *fatwas*. But are they in complete concord with the Qur'an? The verses that I have cited demand that you invite non-hostile people to the path of God by goodly exhortation, peace, mutual respect, and without any force. In addition, they state that you are to deal with them with justice and equity. But the *fatwas* you have cited are diametrically opposed to these Qur'anic instructions! Have the jurists not erred?" They would reply: "We submit to their *fatwas*, for we cannot imagine such a possibility. Thus, there is no alternative other than to attack you." After saying this, they would issue the necessary order to launch an offensive war in order to impose Islam by military force and to reap the reward of jihad!

What would be the response of such jurists when confronted with the strong logic and proofs derived from the Qur'an by the non-hostile unbelievers' leader? It would be none other than to reject all such historical *fatwas* because they have tarnished Islam's image around the world and constitute a devastating blow to its honor and dignity.

This *fatwa*, which is present in the jurisprudential texts and advanced to justify all unjust wars conducted by oppressive rulers, supposedly in the name of Islam, has given the West an effective propaganda tool. Naturally, those who oppose Islam state the following whenever they can: "In Islam, offensive war against peaceful non-Muslim peoples is both permissible and has occurred many times. This is the real Islam, a religion of oppression and anguish which legitimizes savage wars on the basis of *fatwas* while simultaneously proclaiming that it has been misrepresented and stereotyped as a religion of violence." The objective Islam, that which attracted the people's hearts in the past and continues to do so via logic and cogent proofs, is being accused of being thirsty for human blood and for imposing religion by force! Glory be to God!

Jihad is conditional upon the infallible Imam's command

The discussion so far is in accord with both Sunni and Shi'i jurisprudence. One subject matter, however, appears only in the "chapter of jihad" found in Shi'i jurisprudential works. Shi'i jurists have made such a jihad's legitimacy conditional upon the command of the empowered infallible Imam (*mabsut al-yad*). If he has not authorized it, then it would be fundamentally illegitimate to embark upon it. In addition, Shaykh Najafi claims that the relevant *fatwas* are clear about this.[35] In other words, the Imam is the actual leader, ruler, and individual entrusted with implementing all aspects of the society's affairs, such as at the time of Imam 'Ali. To the best of my knowledge, there is no dissent at all on this issue among the Shi'i jurists who agree: The primary jihad is an offensive war against the unbelievers that is conditional upon the infallible Imam's command. A defensive war, however, is not bound by this condition because defense is an unavoidable necessity which must be enforced to repel the evil of the enemy. As the primary jihad is conditional upon the infallible Imam, either he or his appointed deputy must lead it personally.

Source of this idea

A few hadiths on the need for a just ruler to lead a jihad have been attributed to Imams Sadiq and Rida: "Jihad is

---

[35] Najafi, *Jawahir al-kalam*, 21:13 and 14.

obligatory under the command of a just ruler (*imam 'adil*)."[36] It is necessary to note that such hadiths attributed to the Prophet's family began circulating at a time when jihad was declared legitimate and participation was mandatory under the leadership of every oppressive leader. Such hadiths were designed to support the government and therefore were disseminated widely. An oppressive leader who acts according to his own whims and caprice will obviously not hesitate to shed innocent blood, violate ethical norms and values, and conduct the war without regard for justice and equity. The organs of the government of that time relied on hadiths, attributed to the Prophet, which made participation in such undertakings obligatory. Their transmitter is Abu Hurayrah, who is infamous for lying and fabricating hadiths. The text of the hadith is like this: "Jihad is compulsory for everyone under the leadership of every ruler, be he just or corrupt."[37] In such an atmosphere, oppressive rulers would invite contingents of believers to join them under the slogan of "Islamic jihad" with the intention to attack and shed the blood of those who were seeking peace. The infallible Imams, in order to awaken the public declared that "Jihad must be conducted under the leadership of a just ruler (*imam 'adil*)" in an attempt to inform the people of the religious conditions for participating in such a war and to avoid those that were unjust. As such, the *imam 'adil* referred to in these hadiths

---

[36] 'Amili, *Wasa'il al-Shi'ah*, 11:35, hadiths 9 and 10.
[37] Sulayman b. al-Ash'ath al-Sijistani, *Sunan Abi Dawud*, (Beirut: Dar al-fikr, 1990), 1:569, hadith no. 2533.

is to be contrasted with a corrupt and a wretched imam who personified the oppressive ruler or caliph.

Basically, conventional usage of *imam 'adil* in this context is in opposition to *imam ja'ir* or *imam zalim* (unjust or oppressive), not in opposition to an imam who is not *ma'sum* (infallible). Imam 'Ali advised 'Uthman, the third caliph, as follows:

> You should know that among Allah's creatures, the most distinguished person is the just Imam who has been guided (by Allah) and guides others. So, he stands by the recognized ways of the Prophet's behavior and destroys unrecognized innovations. The [Prophet's] ways are clear and have signs, while innovations are also clear and also have signs. Certainly the worst person is the oppressive Imam who has gone astray and through whom others go astray. He destroys the accepted *sunnah* and revives abandoned innovations.[38]

It is clear that the discussion on *imam 'adil* is in opposition to *imam ja'ir,* and not *imam ma'sum* in opposition to *imam ghayr ma'sum* (a non-infallible imam). Thus, once we know why such hadiths appeared, we should not imagine that the referent of *imam 'adil* is *imam ma'sum*.

---

[38] *Nahj al-balaghah*, compiled by al-Sharif al-Radi, trans. Sayed Ali Reza (Rome: European Islamic Cultural Center, 1984), Sermon 163, 330.

But Shi'i jurists have applied *imam 'adil* in these hadiths to the *imam ma'sum*. The source of this equivalence is that in the "Imamate" section of their theological works, they provide a lengthy and elaborate discussion concerning infallibility and agree that the Imam must be infallible. With this mindset and worldview in place, they equated the term *imam 'adil* which appears in the jihad hadiths – to *imam ma'sum*, which appears in their theological works. Thus, they issued a *fatwa* that jihad can be undertaken only with the infallible Imam's consent. According to Shi'i scholars, this issue is so well established that Fayd Kashani says: "Given that the primary jihad has been suspended during the time of the Imam's occultation, we have avoided talking about its conditions and conduct."[39] In other words, a legitimate jihad cannot be launched until this figure reappears and gives the necessary command. As such, there is no reason to enumerate the relevant conditions and conduct. The jihad that he is referring to is the same offensive jihad that Shi'i and Sunni jurists have made lawful in order to impose Islam on unbelievers, because defensive jihad in response to enemy aggression is a perpetual necessity which can never be suspended.

Error in equating *imam 'adil* with *imam ma'sum*

This equivalence is not correct, because a legitimate jihad requires the actual presence of a just leader to conduct it

---

[39] Muhsin al-Fayd al-Kashani, *Tafisr al-safi*, ed. Husayn al-A'lami (Tehran: Maktabah al-Sadr, 1995), 2:73.

in an equitable and just manner, both in relation to his own military forces and also in regards to his enemies, and not to behave as an oppressive commander does. The hadiths that require the commander to be just while conducting the war were issued in response to the fabricated hadiths circulated by the government that mandated participation irrespective of whether the leader was just or not. Thus, they are unrelated to the leader's necessary infallibility.

At times, equivalence is claimed on the assertion that the jurists had reached a consensus, or that there had been no dissent.[40] However, this cannot constitute an independent proof, because the same hadiths have established that equating *imam 'adil* with *imam ma'sum* is a process fraught with difficulty.

What is the merit and benefit of jurists discussing a scenario that can never be realized because, according to them, only the now-occulted, infallible Imam can call for the primary jihad to overpower the enemies? Is not doing so a waste of time and unworthy of *fiqh-e istidlali* (evidentiary jurisprudence)?! It is surprising that among the Shi'i jurists, only Ayatullah Khumayni questioned or hesitated to accept this. According to him, "In this matter, there is scope for discussion and reflection (*bahth wa ta'ammul*)." He talks about this in his *Kitab al-bay'* when dealing with the governance of the jurist.[41] In sum, he

---

[40] Najafi, *Jawahir al-kalam*, 21:13.
[41] Ruhullah al-Musawi al-Khumayni, *Kitab al-bay'* (Qum: Mu'assasah Ismai'liyyan, 1989), 2:496.

opined that there is a likelihood that the command of such an offensive war, the primary form of jihad, may not be limited to the empowered infallible Imam; in fact, it might include the jurisconsult (*wali-ye faqih*) if he has the means to carry out the mission.

Response to the Voice of America

Here, it is appropriate to mention a program broadcast on Thursday, 9 September 1982 called *"Shoma wa ma"* ("You and Us"). While responding to the listener's letters, the host read one in which eighteen questions had been asked, the last of which was:

> Based on the consensus of the Shi'i jurists, jihad must be undertaken only under the infallible Imam's leadership. So how could Ayatullah Khumayni, contrary to this consensus, give a command of jihad and say that 'we must fight against Israel'? Is confronting Israel jihad or defensive war? If it is jihad, then it should not be permissible without the infallible Imam's consent.

The response, according to Ayatullah Khumayni, is that the right of granting permission to fight the unbelievers as the primary jihad, which is claimed to be limited to the person of the infallible Imam, is one that invites further inquiry, analysis, and reflection. It is therefore likely that he considers the jurisconsult to have the same mandate or responsibility as the infallible Imam, because he does not negate this possibility. Furthermore, it is possible that he may have rejected or regarded as unreliable the claimed juristic consensus that declaring jihad is the infallible Imam's exclusive right and responsibility.

In my opinion, however, the response is that in Islam, launching an offensive war against peaceful unbelievers under the slogan of jihad is fundamentally illegitimate, for only self-defense against an aggressive enemy who is actively attacking, has been made religiously mandatory. This is a natural right, and the world accepts it as such. Thus, it is not conditional upon the infallible Imam's permission. But it is necessary, however, that all aspects of a self-defensive war should be in the hands of a leader who is just and God-conscious so that it can be carried out in line with justice and equity. On the strength of this argument, the subject of whether the jurisconsult also enjoys the infallible Imam's right to launch an offensive jihad against hostile unbelievers is negated.

Surprise attack against the unbelievers

In order to "prove" that primary jihad is offensive jihad against the unbelievers, Sunni and Shi'i jurists have attempted to establish two issues by citing the Prophet's practice: (1) a surprise pre-emptive strike is permissible because the Prophet used such a tactic against the unbelieving Banu Mustaliq tribe, and (2) if the invitation to Islam had already reached the unbelievers, then there is no need to invite them again before attacking, since the Prophet did not do so before attacking the Banu Mustaliq.

Jurists have issued rulings on the strength of the hadith related by 'Abdallah b. 'Umar: 'Abdallah b. 'Awn says:

> In a letter to Nafi', the master of Ibn 'Umar, I asked if it was necessary to invite unbelievers to Islam before commencing war against them. He replied: "This was mandatory during the early period of Islam but thereafter was removed, as exhibited in the Prophet's behavior toward the Banu Mustaliq. He attacked them by surprise while they were watering their animals, killed those who fought him, and captured their families. In this event, the Prophet took Juwayriyyah, daughter of Harith (leader of Banu Mustaliq)." Nafi' says: "This story was related to me by 'Abdallah b. 'Umar, who was serving in the army."[42]

I present here some of the *fatwas* issued by Sunni and Shi'i jurists who have relied on this hadith.

Fatwa of Ibn Humam Hanafi

Ibn Humam Hanafi says in *Fath al-Qadir*: "It is not mandatory to issue an invitation to the unbelievers before commencing war in places where the call of Islam has already reached them. This is based on the hadith in *Sahih Muslim* related by 'Abdallah b. 'Awn."[43] Ibn Humam wants to argue that this particular incident constitutes a

---

[42] Ibn Athir, *Jami' al-usul*, 3:205.
[43] Ibn Humam, *Sharh Fath al-qadir*, 5:196.

proof that one can launch an offensive war against unbelievers who are familiar with the invitation to Islam without formally inviting them again.

Fatwa of Shaykh Tusi

Shaykh Tusi, in order to prove that during an offensive war the Muslim leader has a right to undertake a surprise attack, says: "The Muslims' leader has a right to militarily attack the unbelievers by surprise and to kill them because the Prophet did this with the Banu Mustaliq."[44] Seeking to establish and prove that those unbelievers who have already heard the message of Islam do not need to be re-invited before commencing war, he rules: "The Muslim's leader has a right to send out military forces to fight the unbelievers without inviting them to Islam, so long as they are familiar with Islam. He is allowed to kill them in a surprise attack and take them captive, just as the Prophet did with the Banu Mustaliq."[45]

Fatwa of 'Allamah Hilli

'Allamah Hilli allows for this type of attack, provided that the unbelievers to be fought are aware of Islam's basic principles:

> As for those who are aware of Islam and the Prophet's mission, yet did not convert, an

---

[44] Muhammad b. Hasan al-Tusi, *al-Mabsut fi fiqh al-Imamiyyah* (Qum: al-Maktabah al-murtadawiyyah, 1967), 2:11.
[45] Ibid., 2:13.

offensive war may be launched against them without inviting them to Islam. This is because they are aware of the Prophet's invitation, and that his intention was to bring people to embrace Islam. As such, he fought those who did not submit to Islam, and provided safety and security to those who did. These types of unbelievers are categorized as belligerent (*kafir-e harbi*) in the nomenclature of the Muslims and offensive war against them is allowed, because the Messenger initiated offensive war against the Banu Mustaliq when they had no knowledge of such an attack, posed no threat to the Muslims, and were watering their camels.[46]

Fatwa of Shahid II

Shahid II opines:

> The necessity of inviting the unbelievers before initiating war is lifted with regard to those who were invited in a previous war or by some other channel. It is on this basis that the Prophet, without any invitation, fought and annihilated the Banu Mustaliq. Inviting unbelievers to Islam in such a situation is only recommended because Imam 'Ali invited 'Amr b. 'Abdawud and others

---

[46] Hilli, *Tadhkirah al-fuqaha'*, 1:409.

to Islam, even though they had already heard about its call.[47]

Fatwa of Muhammad Hasan al-Najafi (Sahib Jawahir)

Shaykh Najafi writes:

> Shaykh Tusi, Muhaqqiq Hilli, 'Allamah Hilli, Shahid I, Shahid II, and others have made it explicit that the necessity of inviting the unbelievers before initiating war against them is rescinded, provided that they have already heard the call in a previous war or through some other means. The other proof is, as some have recorded, that the Prophet attacked the Banu Mustaliq and caused them to perish while they were in a state of peace and watering their camels. It is likely that there is no dissent on this matter.[48]

It is clear that the aforementioned scholars have attributed to the Prophet two practices on the basis of this particular hadith: (1) that he launched a surprise attack against the Banu Mustaliq and (2) that they were not invited to Islam before being attacked.

It is necessary to verify this hadith's authenticity. This can be done by consulting the relevant historical sources. The most comprehensive source on this event is found in the

---

[47] Shahid II, *Sharh al-lum'ah*, 1:257.
[48] Najafi, *Jawahir al-kalam*, 21:53.

Maghazi of Waqidi, who specialized in recording the Prophet's battles. He states:

> The Banu Mustaliq of the Khuza'a, allies of the Banu Mudlij, were camping around al-Fur'. Their leader and master, al-Harith b. Abi Dirar, had gone to his people and those who had power over him from the Bedouin, and invited them to fight the Messenger of God. They bought horses and weapons and prepared to march against the Messenger of God. Riders began to arrive from their region and inform him about their march. This reached the Messenger of God, and he sent Burayda b. al-Husayb al-Aslami to verify the information. He sought the Prophet's permission to speak freely, and the Prophet permitted him to do so.
>
> Burayda set out until he arrived at their water wells. He found a misled people who had rallied and come together. They asked, "Who is the man?" He replied, "A man from you. I arrived for what reached me about your gathering for this man. I will march with my people and those who obey me, and our hands will be one until we destroy him." Al-Harith b. Abi Dirar said, "We are with you. Hasten to us." Burayda said, "I will ride now and bring you a group of tough men from my people who will obey me." They rejoiced at this news. Burayda then returned to the Messenger of God and informed him about the people.

The Messenger of God summoned his people, informed them of this latest news, and the people hastened to set out...

Reaching al-Muraysi', the Messenger of God alighted at the water well where a leather tent was erected for him ... He arranged his Companions in rows, he handed the banner of the Muhajirun to Abu Bakr, and the banner of the Ansar to Sa'd b. 'Ubada. Some say the banner of the Muhajirun was with 'Ammar b. Yasir. Then the Prophet commanded 'Umar b. al-Khattab to call out to the people, "Say there is no God but Allah and protect your souls and your property." 'Umar did so, but they refused.

The first to aim an arrow was a man from the Banu Mustaliq. The Muslims aimed arrows for a while. Then the Messenger of God commanded his Companions to attack. They did so as a single man, and not one of the Banu Mustaliq escaped. Some were killed and the rest were taken captive. The Messenger of God captured men, women, and children. Cattle and sheep were plundered. Only one Muslim man was killed.

... Ibn 'Umar used to relate that when the Prophet attacked the Banu Mustaliq, they were unaware. Their cattle were quenching their thirst at the water well when he killed their warriors and captured their children.[49]

After relating this incident, Waqidi mentions that this report "is not reliable, in our estimation." Instead, he favored the one that the Banu Mustaliq had made full preparations to fight the Prophet.[50] As such, the Prophet's military preparations were defensive and designed to forestall the enemy's attack, not to initiate the battle or to launch a surprise attack. Accordingly, Waqidi states that 'Abdallah b. 'Umar's report should be considered unacceptable and the jurists' deductions derived from it be considered unacceptable as well. Moreover, Waqidi recorded that based on the Prophet's instruction, 'Umar invited the Banu Mustaliq to Islam but they refused.

Cause of surprise and perplexity

It is a source of surprise and perplexity as to why the jurists relied upon this weak report and invoked it to issue a legal ruling while ignoring that of Waqidi, who is a thorough and reliable historian. His work was accessible, and they were certainly aware of it. They also had information that Shafi'i, in his *Umm,* along with Ibn Hisham's *Sirah,* Ibn Sa'd's *Tabaqat,* and Tabari's *Ta'rikh,* had all certified the statements attributed to Waqidi. Had they relied on these sources, they would not have attributed such inappropriate acts to the Prophet!

---

[49] Waqidi, *Kitab al-maghazi,* 198-99.
[50] Ibid.

It can be deduced from Ibn Humam Hanafi's earlier statement that the Sunni jurists, without any hesitation, had begun to rely upon this weak statement of 'Abdallah b. 'Umar regarding the Banu Musataliq. This is perhaps because the oppressive government, seeking to legitimize its offensive warfare and oppression, had already spread it as widely as possible. As such, the *fatwa* came to be regarded as an undisputed and uncontested legal ruling! In addition, the fact that he was Caliph 'Umar's son perhaps encouraged its acceptance!

But why did Shaykh Tusi, a Shi'i scholar, rely upon it to issue a legal ruling on such a sensitive issue, even though the works of Waqidi and other reliable historical works were accessible to him?! Was it because the Sunnis' jurisprudence and legal rulings had gained such dominance over the religious seminaries that even someone like Shaykh Tusi could not escape their dominance and gain enough intellectual freedom to exercise independent *ijtihad*? Such a question is not far-fetched; in fact, to a certain extent it seems quite normal that a persecuted minority group, whether it likes it or not, is pushed in the direction of following the majority. A minority jurist is certainly no exception in this regard. Thus, Shaykh Tusi came under this dominant Sunni *fatwa's* influence and left it as a legacy for posterity. His successors, since they trusted the integrity of his scholarship, adopted his opinion and followed him up until the time of Shaykh Najafi, who was prompted to say: "Perhaps there is no dissent on this subject matter."[51]

'Allamah Hilli's portrayal of Muhammad

It is necessary to pause and reflect on 'Allamah Hilli's previously mentioned opinion: "As for those who are aware of Islam and the Prophet's mission, and in spite of this did not convert, offensive war against them is permissible without inviting them to Islam." Would Muhammad really give an ultimatum to either submit to Islam or face immediate military attack? Does 'Allamah Hilli characterize him in such a manner? Which relevant historical texts and sources portray the Prophet in such a manner? No such reliable source is available. Is it possible to believe that the Prophet himself would not act according to the teachings of the Qur'an, which encourages believers to deal kindly and justly with non-hostile unbelievers? Moreover, would he ignore such verses as: "There is no compulsion in religion: true guidance has become distinct from error" (Q. 2:256), and, "Say, 'Now the truth has come from your Lord: let those who wish to believe in it do so, and let those who wish to reject it do so" (Q. 18:29)?

With Makkah lying at his feet and enjoying unparalleled power, the Prophet did not say to even one person "convert to Islam or face death;" rather, he gave the unbelievers the option to retain their own convictions.

---

[51] Najafi, *Jawahir al-kalam*, 21:53.

How could one possibly imagine that such a person would warn his people to either submit to Islam or else face a military confrontation in which their blood would be shed?! Glory be to God!

No one argues that 'Allamah Hilli made these statements on the basis of historical reports, because no such thing exists in the historical annals. But then how is it possible for him to make such claims that contradict the facts and distort the Prophet's compassionate and people-friendly visage into one that is so austere, rude, and merciless that he would impose Islam at the point of sword?!

In my estimation, 'Allamah did not want to rely upon historical sources to make a historical assertion; rather, he sought a historical conclusion from the legal judgment derived by jurists from 'Abdallah b. 'Umar's report that those unbelievers already aware of Islam could be attacked by surprise. This legal judgment was extrapolated to "prove" that the Prophet would first invite people to embrace Islam and then initiate an offensive war if they refused to do so. Even though this historical deduction actually emanated from a legal subject matter, both the ensuing legal judgment and the historical matter from which it is extracted must be considered as null and void since the proof of this legal issue is based on an unreliable report.

Were the people of Ta'if all massacred?

Shaykh Tusi, in line with his opinion on the Banu Mustaliq incident, has a similar opinion regarding the Prophet's encircling of the fortress in Ta'if:

> When an imam enters a town, he has the right to besiege it and prevent anyone from entering or exiting because the Prophet encircled the people of Ta'if. He also has the right to set up and use mangonels, to destroy the walls and the houses of the residents while they are inhabited, and to engage in a massacre because this is how the Prophet acted with the people of Ta'if. If there are no Muslims in the besieged city, then he has a right to pummel them with the mangonel, even if women and children are present, because this is how the Prophet behaved with the people of Ta'if. He is also entitled to flood the place with water to drown them or to use the mangonel, fire, snakes, scorpions, or anything else that would be to their loss.[52]

Anyone who reads this report would be left with no doubt that the Prophet had destroyed these houses via mangonels while the people were still inside them, and then massacred the women and children. This report has been taken from imam Shafi'i's *Umm,* wherein he says:

---

[52] Tusi, *Mabsut,* 2:11.

Whenever the enemy has sought refuge and protection in the mountain, fortress, ditch, or any other place, one can use the mangonel for attacking them with fire, snakes, scorpions, and any such thing that would lead to their loss, or sink them in water even if there are women and children. The proof and evidence for this is that the Prophet used the mangonel against the people of Ta'if, even though there were women and children among them.[53]

We can gather from the above that Shaykh Tusi was influenced by Sunni jurisprudence on a number of issues and issued legal opinions which accorded with Sunni thought. In this case, he relied upon imam Shafi'i, who, along with Sunni scholars, had relied upon the fabricated report attributed 'Abdallah b. 'Umar.

It is here necessary to interrogate whether that which imam Shafi'i and his followers, among them Shaykh Tusi, claim is correct or not. We intend to do this by referring to the historical accounts dealing with the battle of Hunayn and the siege of Ta'if:

1. After the conquest of Makkah, the Hawazin and Thaqif tribes prepared a large army, commanded by Malik b. 'Awf Nasri, to attack the Muslims. To repel them, the Prophet assembled a force and

---

[53] Shafi'i, *Kitab al-umm*, 4:243.

moved toward Hunayn, wherein he defeated the enemy. As such, this action was purely defensive.

2. The Prophet encircled the fortress of Ta'if, which housed belligerent individuals who had suffered defeat and sought refuge in it. During the siege, he resorted to various tactical measures, hoping thereby to minimize the loss in order to subdue the enemy. For example:

    (a)   The Muslims tried to drill a hole in the fortress wall, which caused those inside to climb up the wall and drop scraps of hot iron on them, which burned their leather garments and injured a number of them. When the Muslims retreated, the people in the fort shot arrows at them; a number of them were martyred. In sum, this strategy did not produce a positive outcome for the Muslims.[54]

    (b)   In order to force the enemy to surrender, the Prophet gave a command to destroy the grape vines from which the fruit had already been picked, but the inhabitants of Ta'if protested: "'O

---

[54] Waqidi, *Kitab al-maghazi*, 455.

Muhammad, why are you cutting our wealth? Indeed, you will take it if you are victorious against us. And, indeed, you will put it down to God and the relatives as you claim!' The Messenger of God said, 'Indeed, I can put it down to God and the relatives.' So the Messenger of God left it."[55]

(c)   The Prophet ordered the palace of Malik b. 'Awf, the enemy commander, to be burned down after ensuring that it was vacant.[56] Perhaps this was done to reduce the tyrannical power of this aggressive commander and his followers, as this severe economic loss must have demoralized them and prevented it from becoming a stronghold. This is an appropriate and proportionate punishment for the arrogant commander who, without any cause or justification, had gathered a mighty force to kill Muslims.

---

[55] Ibid.
[56] Ibid., 453.

(d)   Outside of the fortress was a castle surrounded by walls. The Prophet told its owner, a person from the Thaqif tribe: "Either come out of the garden or we will burn it down." The man did not come out, and so they burnt it down (or probably just the door).[57]

If the owner had come out, he would have been taken captive. In addition, he could have been a good source for intelligence. But because he did not come out, in all likelihood they burnt down the door to see what was going on inside and to prevent it from being used as a safe haven for defense.

(e)   The Prophet's herald called out: "Every slave who comes out of the fort and joins us will be freed." More than ten slaves accepted this offer. The Prophet placed each one under a Muslim who was responsible for supervising their learning of the Qur'an and the Sunnah. Thereafter, when the Thaqif tribe embraced Islam, their

---

[57] Ibid.

previous masters asked the Prophet to let them go home. He did not permit them to do so.[58]

The slaves' defection was an economic and a moral blow against the aggressors, for the Muslims benefited from the information they provided about what was going on inside the fortress.

The Prophet implemented these tactical measures during his siege of Ta'if, which was housing people who had aggressed against the Muslims. After a few days, people began discussing whether to continue or lift the siege. Ultimately, the majority chose the second option and the Prophet gave the command to depart.

No unbeliever was killed by the mangonel

In spite of what the historians have written, such as: "The Prophet gave the directive to use the mangonel during the siege of Ta'if," or, "Muslims, on the basis of the Prophet's directive, struck the fort of Ta'if,"[59] no historian has recorded that anyone in Ta'if was killed by mangonel,

---

[58] Ibid, 456.
[59] Ibn Hisham, *The Life of Muhammad*, 589.

even though historians have mentioned the precise details of the battle of Hunayn and the siege of Ta'if. For instance, during the battle of Hunayn, only four people on the Prophet's side died; seventy to one hundred members of the enemy forces were killed. During the siege of Ta'if, only twelve Muslims were martyred. In addition, many of the other events which occurred during the siege are detailed, such as names of those who changed sides and later became Muslims. However, no historian has written that even one person from Ta'if was killed by mangonel at the Prophet's directive. Only one person who had killed a Muslim by spear was arrested by the victim's brother. The Prophet, adhering to the tradition of *qisas* (equal retaliatory punishment), ordered his execution.[60]

It is possible that imam Shafi'i deduced, based on the historical account, that since during this siege the Messenger of God had told his men to use the mangonel, undoubtedly the people's houses were demolished while they were inside, and that this was enough to allow for the massacre of women and children. Permission to drown and torch their opponents was probably added based on analogy. It is indeed very strange that imam Shafi'i would permit human beings, even women and children, to be burned! And more bizarre is that Shaykh Tusi agreed!

Installing the mangonel and using it to hurl stones in a way designed to prevent injury to anyone can constitute a form of a military threat. By inspiring fear, it could

---

[60] Waqidi, *Kitab al-maghazi*, 454.

prompt the hostile forces inside the fort to surrender and thereby prevent everyone, especially the women and children, from being hurt. It is known that the Prophet, unless it was absolutely necessary, forbade the killing of anyone – especially of those who were innocent. During the siege, he acted in the same manner, with the result that not one aggressor was killed.

Accordingly, as the statements of imam Shafi'i and Shaykh Tusi cannot be sustained on the basis of any historical proof, they must be rejected. Perhaps it is from these types of incidents that the jurists developed the idea that unbelievers, along with their women and children, had no inherent right to life. We need to revise and correct this opinion to reflect what the Qur'an actually says: "He [God] does not forbid you to deal kindly and justly with anyone who has not fought you for your faith or driven you out of your homes. God loves those who are just" (Q. 60:8).

Mandatory offensive war: Once a year

We mentioned earlier that the jurists viewed offensive war against peaceful unbelievers as mandatory because, essentially, God demands this just as He mandates prayers, fasting, and hajj. As a result, if prayers are obligatory every day, if fasting is mandated during Ramadan every year, and if hajj is required once during one's lifetime, then what about jihad? Is it obligatory every month, every year, or once in a lifetime? If one were to respond on the basis of reality, jihad would be obligatory only when the enemy attacks; however, the jurists opined that the Divine Legislator mandates offensive war against peaceful unbelievers. Thus, Muslims are obliged to establish this obligation, just as they are to establish prayers, fasting, and hajj. There is one problem here, however: neither the Qur'an nor the Sunnah contain any proof that could be invoked to support this position, because both of them prohibit such an offensive war. Nevertheless, the jurists proclaimed that "offensive jihad against peaceful unbelievers, just like prayers and fasting, is obligatory." Given this, they had to search for a way to specify when and how many times the unbelievers could be attacked. The first person to dwell upon this and codify it in *fiqh* was imam Shafi'i.

Fatwa of imam Shafi'i

In his *Umm,* imam Shafi'i exerts himself to extract this legal judgment from the Prophet's Sunnah:

> If the Muslims are strong, they should not allow a year to pass by without warring against the polytheists who are surrounded by Muslim lands. If it is possible for them, I would prefer that they should war as many times as possible against them without putting the Muslims in any kind of jeopardy. At a minimum, the caliph must not allow a year to elapse without fighting, for if he were to do so the obligation of jihad would be suspended without a justification during the course of a year. I say this because from the time that

jihad was mandated upon him, the Messenger of God would initiate one or two wars each year, either by himself or through somebody else. Sometimes, time would elapse during which he would neither go to war nor send a contingent to fight them.[61]

In order to establish his opinion, Shafi'i cited the Prophet's practice. But when did the Prophet ever instruct the Muslims to do so? Shafi'i himself says: "Sometimes, time would elapse during which he would neither go to war nor send a contingent to fight the unbelievers."

Whenever the Prophet's enemies conducted aggression against him, he reacted in ways designed to defend the Muslims, either with his own presence or through his appointee. Sometimes this occurred one, two, or more times a year; at other times, no incidents occurred for a long period. Thus, his response was contingent upon his enemies' hostile aggression, meaning that at no time did he launch an offensive war against peaceful unbelievers. If someone were to be asked: "How many times in a year do you visit a physician?" he would respond: "Whenever I am sick," because visiting a physician is, in itself, not mandatory. The Prophet's wars were of the same nature. Offensive war is inherently not obligatory and the Prophet, just as 'Allamah Muhammad Jawad Balaghi and Shaykh Muhammad 'Abduh have said, and as the

---

[61] Shafi'i, *Kitab al-umm*, 4:168.

historical facts reveal, only resorted to self-defensive warfare.

Basing ourselves on the Prophet's practice, it is unambiguously clear that one cannot allege that he ever mandated at least one annual offensive against peaceful unbelievers. What prompted Shafi'i to insist upon his opinion so strongly was that, as mentioned earlier, he regarded the restrictive verses that made war against the unbelievers conditional upon the latter being the initiator as having been abrogated. Consequently, by relying upon absolute verses on jihad he concluded that offensive war is obligatory, and thus, that its timing and frequency must be determined. And since the Qur'an and the Sunnah contain no proof to sustain this position, he had no alternative but to insist with vehemence and attach himself to the Prophet's practice, even though it provides no supporting evidence! If he had adopted the right course from the beginning instead of considering the restrictive verses abrogated, he could have used those very verses to rule that offensive war against peaceful unbelievers is not permissible. But whenever the enemy aggresses against the Muslims or is on the verge of doing so, initiating jihad becomes obligatory. Consequently, he would not have to rely upon unacceptable proofs garnered from the Prophet's practice to specify the jihad's timing and frequency, and thereby leave an incorrect opinion for future jurists.

Incidentally, since Shafi'i brings into the discourse the Abbasid caliphs and their war-related responsibilities, might one not speculate that he was forced to rule in favor of the caliphs who were already embroiled in offensive wars? One cannot negate this probability. And if this was actually the case, politics had an impact on the issuance of his legal judgment.

Another point to keep in mind is that 'Umar, the second caliph, used to send out a contingent of soldiers every year for war.[62] It is likely that his established practice also influenced the issuance of imam Shafi'i's *fatwa*. Yet this particular *fatwa*, which is not acceptable under any circumstances, was also recorded and codified as part of *fiqh*. Over time, it became unchallengeable at the religious seminaries and dominated that culture to such an extent that Shaykh Tusi was unable to free himself from the ensuing hegemonic discourse. He followed the dominant *fiqh* of the time and gave an identical *fatwa* without even interrogating or analyzing it!

Fatwa of Shaykh Tusi

Shaykh Tusi writes: "It is obligatory upon the Imam to engage in a war against the unbelievers once a year, either by himself at the helm, or by appointing someone else with a contingent of soldiers so that the institution of jihad is not abandoned."[63] Acts that are obligatory and have been demanded by God (e.g., prayers and fasting) can be ended. But this is not possible for such things as defensive war, which is contingent upon the enemy's actual

---

[62] Ibn Athir, *Jami' al-usul*, 3:223.
[63] Tusi, *Mabsut*, 2:2.

aggression or preparedness for it. But those jurists who favored attacking peaceful unbelievers viewed it as an act of worship and thus essentially mandatory, as is the case with prayers and fasting. As such, Shaykh asserts: "At the bare minimum, the Imam is obliged to initiate a war once every year. The higher the number of military engagements, the greater will be the virtue because jihad is a collective responsibility. Thus, naturally its virtue would also increase in direct proportion."[64]

Clearly, the same *fatwa* of Shafi'i has entered into Shaykh Tusi's work without being subjected to any scrutiny or analysis. He only replaced *caliph* with *Imam*. He means the infallible Imam, because Shi'i jurists regard offensive war as conditional upon this person's command, for only he has the capacity to engage in such a war. Later jurists who came under his influence adopted his position and recorded the same legal opinion in their own jurisprudential works.

Fatwa of Muhaqqiq Hilli

In his *Shara'i' al-Islam*, Muhaqqiq Hilli states:

> Regarding those whom Muslims are obliged to engage in war, they must fight them, repel their aggression, or force them to convert. If the unbelievers start the war, then it is obligatory for the Muslims to fight them. If they refrain from doing so, then in this situation war is obligatory

---

[64] Ibid., 2:10.

only to the extent of the Muslim's capability and, at a minimum, once a year. If public welfare demands a peace agreement with them, then reaching one is allowed.[65]

Thus, he is also following Shaykh Tusi's opinion, just as the latter followed the opinion of Shafi'i, without engaging in any critical analysis.

Two points are worthy of mention here: (1) according to him, war can be employed to convert people, which is equivalent to imposing Islam by force, and (2) that, as he says: "If the unbelievers refrain from war, then it is obligatory to fight them to the extent possible." Clearly, he views the launch of an offensive war to convert unbelievers as obligatory.

After Muhaqqiq, other jurists relied on Shaykh Tusi's *fatwa* in their own works, just as Shaykh Tusi had relied on Shafi'i in issuing his legal opinion. In addition to accepting this *fatwa's* validity, 'Allamah Hilli attempted to provide proofs and evidence to justify it.

Fatwa of 'Allamah Hilli

'Allamah Hilli writes:

If the unbelievers are on their own land and have no intention of fighting the Muslims, then going to

---

[65] Abu al-Qasim Ja'far b. al-Hasan (Muhaqqiq al-Hilli), *Shara'i' al-Islam fi masa'il al-halal wa al-haram*, ed. Sayyid Sadiq Shirazi (Tehran: Intisharat al-Istiqlal, 1988), 1:235.

war against them is a collective obligation (*wajib-e kefa'i*) and not individually obligatory (*wajib-e 'ayni*). This must be done at least once a year, and its virtue increases in direct proportion to the higher number of wars. The Messenger of God fought the unbelievers every year, as indicated by battle of Badr in 624, Uhud in 625, Dhat al-riqa' in 626, Ditch (Khandaq) in 627, war against the Banu Mustaliq in 628, Khaybar in 629, the conquest of Makkah in 630, and Tabuk in 631.[66]

I object to this dominant juristic opinion on the grounds that these jurists have assumed that the principal and primary jihad (*jihad-e asli*) is against the unbelievers, whereas the Prophet's wars were defensive in nature. In such a situation, how can one cite his practice, which was always based on self-defense, as proof for offensive war?

At Badr, the Prophet did his best to prevent the outbreak of war. Yet when the unbelievers rejected his proposal and attacked, he had no alternative but to defend his community. Likewise, at Uhud, the enemy started the attack and the Prophet only defended himself. All of his other wars were similarly defensive in nature. Thus during the first year after the hijrah, there was no fighting because the enemy did not attack. Given this fact, how can any jurist claim that the Prophet planned to engage in a war at least once a year? Clearly, his battles were

---

[66] Hilli, *Tadhkirah al-fuqaha'*, 1:406.

launched only in self-defense and cannot be cited to prove this particular obligation.

Incidentally, 'Allamah has said: "The war of the Ditch (Khandaq) took place in 627 and the war against Banu Mustaliq in 628," whereas Waqidi states that both of them occurred in 627 and the war against Banu Mustaliq took place before the war of Khandaq.[67] Accordingly, there were two defensive wars in one year because the enemies engaged in aggression twice.

The reality is that 'Allamah Hilli also fell under the influence of the eminent Shaykh Tusi, who had accepted the *fatwa* of Shafi'i. 'Allamah desired to substantiate it by invoking as proof the Prophet's practice of fighting the unbelievers once a year. However, it has become evident that such reasoning, and the proof advanced are both faulty and lacking.

Fatwa of Shahid I and Shahid II

Shahid I and Shahid II have said in *Lum'ah* and its commentary:

> Jihad is a collective obligation to the extent that it is necessary. It must be conducted at least once a year, based on the evidence of 'When the [four] forbidden months are over, wherever you find the polytheists, kill them, seize them, besiege them, ambush them — but if they turn [to God],

---

[67] Waqidi, *Kitab al-maghazi*, 198, 215-16.

maintain the prayer, and pay the prescribed alms, let them go on their way, for God is most forgiving and merciful' (Q.9:5), which states that jihad is conditional upon the passage of the four forbidden months. This obviously occurs only once every year. However, the proof and mode of reasoning is open to debate and discussion.[68]

It appears that these two scholars envision that this obligation is beyond dispute; rather they have objections as to the evidence and proof advanced to substantiate this position.

The argument, based on Qur'an 9:5, first appears in the discourse of 'Allamah Hilli, in his *Tadhkirah*. The authors of the *Sharh Lum'ah* have presented the same proofs, and have stated that there is scope for debate and discussion on this matter. They do not, however, provide any details.

But the aforementioned Qur'anic verse pertains only to those unbelievers who had broken the treaty and were given four months to depart: "You [polytheists] may move freely about the land for four months" (Q. 9:2). This verse's apparent meaning is that these four months are consecutive and, as such, it cannot refer to the four sacred but non-consecutive months (viz., Dhulqa'dah, Dhulhijjah, Muharram, and Rajab). Moreover, the Qur'an states: "When the [four] forbidden months are over" (Q. 9:5), thereby indicating the end of this period of grace. If

---

[68] Shahid II, *Sharh al-lum'ah*, 1:255.

they still insist on fighting and not honoring their agreements, then the Muslims must pummel them with military force.

As a result, the consecutive "four forbidden months" mentioned in this verse are not the same as the sacred months (viz., Dhulqaʻdah, Dhulhijjah, Muharram, and Rajab), which are non-consecutive and thus one cannot say that: "In every year when the four sacred months have elapsed, offensive war against the unbelievers is obligatory at least once a year."

ʻAllamah Hilli, who had already accepted the obligation of an annual offensive war, was searching for evidence and proof to substantiate this claim. At times, he relied upon the Prophet's (already refuted) practice of launching an annual offensive war; at other times, he attached himself to Qur'an 9:5, which is irrelevant to this discourse. The right course from the outset would have been for him to reject this notion and thus obviate the need to resort to evidence that neither validates nor proves his point.

Clearly, Shahid I and Shadid II accepted the inherent necessity for this type of offensive war once a year due to their following the opinion of Shaykh Tusi, who had emulated the *fatwa* of imam Shafiʻi. As demonstrated above, the latter's *fatwa* has no connection to any proof or evidence from jurisprudence and *ijtihad*.

Fatwa of al-Muhaqqiq al-Karaki (Muhaqqiq Thani) (d. 1530 or 1534)

In his *Jami' al-maqasid,* which is a commentary on *Qawa'id* of 'Allamah, Muhaqqiq Thani says:

> Jihad is obligatory once a year unless there is a justifiable reason, in which case it is sometimes not mandatory. On occasion, it is obligatory to go to war more than once in a year. The evidence for this is based on text (*nass*) and consensus (*ijma'*).[69]

Muhaqqiq Thani, who saw no dissent among the earlier jurists, accepted the *fatwa* which was in circulation at the time on offensive war, however, it was better if he had not accepted it uncritically: "Evidence for this judgment is based on text and consensus." The "text" is Qur'an 9:5, which 'Allamah Hilli had invoked as proof to substantiate his position even though, as demonstrated above, this verse is irrelevant to this legal judgment. By "consensus," he means that all of the jurists from Shaykh Tusi onward gave the same *fatwa*, which can be traced back to Shafi'i. Accordingly, no binding *ijma'* can be used as a proof.

---

[69] Al-Muhaqqiq al-Karaki, *Jami' al-maqasid* (Qum: Mu'assasah Al al-Bayt, 1987), 3:365.

Fatwa of Muhammad Hasan al-Najafi (Sahib Jawahir)

Shaykh Najafi writes:

> Shaykh Tusi, 'Allamah, Shahid I, Shahid II, and Muhaqqiq Karaki have recorded that, at a minimum, jihad must be performed once a year, and the latter has claimed that a consensus was already obtained on this issue. The primary proof for this legal judgment is the same consensus, if it truly was a consensus, and not Qur'an 9:5. Thus, as you can see, these evidences and proofs are open to contestation and scrutiny.[70]

Najafi does not challenge the primary obligation of fighting the unbelievers once a year; rather, he disputes the validity of the Qur'anic verse advanced as proof by 'Allamah Hilli. Then he says: "The primary proof for this issue is consensus, if it truly was a consensus," although he knew that the *ijma'* on this matter was absent because Shaykh Tusi had originally taken this *fatwa* from imam Shafi'i, whose legal opinion and proofs are totally unacceptable.

At times, Najafi's opinion can become a source of confusion and perplexity because of his statement: "The primary proof for this issue is consensus, if it truly was a consensus." This implies a sense of hesitancy on his part to confirm the presence of *ijma'*. If it cannot be

---

[70] Najafi, *Jawahir al-kalam*, 21:10 and 11.

established with certainty, then, in his estimation there is no evidence and proof to substantiate the issue of offensive war, because he rejects the Qur'anic verse cited by 'Allamah Hilli. As such, this predominant legal *fatwa* would, according to him, remain unsubstantiated and therefore negated. I do not know if this supposition can be attributed to Najafi or not.

The necessity of revoking the predominant *fatwa*

The jurists have stated that Muslims are obliged, based on textual evidence and consensus, to launch an offensive war once a year even if the unbelievers are not hostile and at peace with the Muslims. If this were really the case, then one would expect Imam 'Ali, during his short caliphate, to obey it. And yet he did not. Is not this proof that God did not demand such an activity, because if He had, surely the Imam would have acted upon it?

If the jurists have no response to this question, then the equitable thing to do is to distance themselves from this *fatwa*, and to ensure that Islam's reputation from this point onward is no longer tarnished by its custodians' claim that they are obliged to attack and kill peaceful unbelievers. This *fatwa* has been – and remains – a source of irreparable damage to Islam's honor and stature, as well as an injustice that the jurists have inadvertently imposed upon this divine religion!

Reason for Solomon's military warning

It has been demonstrated that imposing Islam by military force is unacceptable, for the Qur'an proclaims that people must be offered guidance in the best manner through wisdom, goodly exhortation, and logical proofs. But what about Solomon's military threat to the rulers of Sheba? Could this be construed as desiring to impose religion on them by force? The rulers rejected his invitation to visit him and instead sent him presents. But he refused to accept their gifts: "Go back to your people: we shall certainly come upon them with irresistible forces, and drive them, disgraced and humbled, from their land" (Q. 27:37). What else could this threat represent but imposing faith via military force?

In order to obtain a response, a sound understanding of the incident's context and circumstances is necessary, for how else can one surmise the purpose of his threat and intimidation? In short, Solomon, with the hoopoe bird's help, learns of the existence of Sheba, its queen and council of rulers, and their situation from all aspects. In his report, the hoopoe relates:

> "I have learned something you did not know: I come to you from Sheba with firm news. I found a woman ruling over the people, [a woman] who has been given a share of everything – she has a magnificent throne – [but] I found that she and her people worshipped the sun instead of God. Satan has made their deeds seem alluring to them and

diverted them from the right path: they cannot find the right path. Should they not worship God, who brings forth what is hidden in the heavens and earth and knows both what you people conceal and what you declare? He is God, there is no god but Him, the Lord of the mighty throne." Solomon said, "We shall see whether you are telling the truth or lying. Take this letter of mine and deliver it to them, then withdraw and see what answer they send back." The Queen of Sheba said, "Counselors, a gracious letter has been delivered to me. It is from Solomon, and it says, 'In the name of God, the Lord of Mercy, the Giver of Mercy, do not put yourselves above me, and come to me in submission to God.'" She said, "Counselors, give me your counsel in the matter I now face: I only ever decide on matters in your presence." They replied, "We possess great force and power in war, but you are in command, so consider what orders to give us." She said, "Whenever kings go into a city, they ruin it and humiliate its leaders – that is what they do – but I am going to send them a gift, then see what answer my envoy brings back." When her envoy came to Solomon, Solomon said, "What! Are you offering me wealth? What God has given me is better than what He has given you, though you rejoice in this gift of yours. Go back to your people: we shall certainly come upon them with irresistible forces, and drive them, disgraced and humbled, from their land" (Q. 27:22-37).

Solomon, now aware of Sheba's political, social, and religious culture, sent them a respectful invitation starting with the *basmalah* (i.e., in the Name of God, the Most Compassionate, the Most Merciful). He cautioned them not to consider themselves better than him and to come to him with honor and respect. Upon receiving his letter, the queen consulted her council of rulers as to how she should respond. Finally, she opted to send gifts to Solomon.

A few points must be noted here to discover the reality, purpose, and goals of Solomon's threat:

1. Based on the information he had received, Solomon gathered that Sheba's government was despotic and tyrannical, ruled by a woman who exercised full control and monopolized all power. Thus, the people had no say in administering the kingdom's or their own affairs, and so had no choice but to tolerate oppression, discrimination, and force without raising their voice. As such, they were reduced to a life of slavery and enjoyed no scope for intellectual freedom, action, and movement toward perfection. The government even dictated their beliefs and mode of worship.

2. Solomon had invited the council's members, as opposed to the people, to present themselves to him because the sources of the peoples' afflictions

were the council and its tyrannical government. If there is hope for a genuine reform, one must begin with the key government figures. Until that is done, there is no possibility of any reform at the lower echelon of society. Thus, his invitation was intended to bring about this reform, which could then lead to social reform.

3. Solomon demanded that the council and especially the queen, present themselves humbly and respectfully, without making any claims of superiority over him. If they failed to do so, he would use his military force to expel them in a humiliating manner. In other words, he threatened to expel the council in order to remove the root cause of affliction so that the imprisoned and oppressed people could live in a land without dictators and oppressors. Thus, their current lack of freedom would be replaced with a life of prosperity and success.

4. Solomon did not say anything about imposing the creed of God's oneness with force, or talk about the existing belief system, because they were irrelevant. After he had expelled the council members responsible for the despotic government, the people would live in a free environment and therefore be able to talk about religion in an open environment. As they would then be following the truth, there was no need for him to say that "I

would like to impose the religion under the rubric of jihad," as the jurists have argued.

5. Solomon was aiming for something dictated by human conscience, namely, to liberate the oppressed. If people are imprisoned, smothered by a tyrant, and are not strong enough to overthrow them, whereas someone else can do this successfully, then conscience dictates that such a person has a rational responsibility to do so. The newly freed people can then freely chart their own future for a prosperous life and begin to move toward the path of perfection. This is why Solomon, after he learned about the oppressed people of Sheba, decided to intervene. He saw it as his moral duty to remove the tyrannical government and thereby free Sheba's people from injustice and persecution.

6. He did not intend to act upon his threat to subdue Sheba via military force, but to use it as a way to bring about reform. In other words, the underlying wisdom was the threat itself and not its actualization, because the available contextual evidence shows that the council of rulers voluntarily came to see Solomon. Once aware of his unparalleled power, there was no need to dispatch his military forces. As such, they came humbly and respectfully, thereby beginning the processes of freeing the kingdom's people and

reforming their political, social, and even doctrinal concepts.

7. Solomon thought of a plan that would allow the queen and the council members to witness his divinely blessed authority. Its miraculous nature to bring about a radical transformation in their souls would enable them to accept the truth with humility and dignity, to dissociate themselves from sun worship, and accept monotheism. As such, when they were still on the road, one of Solomon's followers acted upon the latter's directive to fetch the queen's throne via divine power. When she presented herself at court and saw her throne, she recognized it instantly, as she had made some changes to it. This strengthened her conviction of God's divine assistance to Solomon, and thus she said: "Before we were not aware of the grandeur and truthfulness of this pious man, but are now prepared to submit to him." In his presence, she repented: "My Lord, I have wronged myself. I devote myself, with Solomon, to God, the Lord of the Worlds" (Q. 27:44).

This revolution in her thinking and belief system, due to the grace of Solomon's plan, impacted her soul, as well as those of the council members, and caused them to enter into a new world, one infused with light and luminosity. As a result, they attached themselves to the path of true prosperity.

Her statement: "God, I had wronged myself" reveals that the most serious wrong was the despotic and arrogant government's having robbed the people of their freedom and personal opinion. But now she, along with the delegation, had voluntarily approached the sphere of the Divine to confess to their sins and change the course of their lives. As a result, the people could now benefit from kingdom's existing resources. This is what Solomon had desired to achieve.

8. His approach is identical to that of the rest of God's messengers, including that of Prophet Muhammad. Just as the Prophet and the Qur'an, in harmony with one's intellect and conscience, do not allow Islam to be imposed by military force, Solomon likewise used the same approach. Thus, it is not possible to imagine that he was threatening to impose monotheism by force. Solomon resorted to wisdom and the best means to demolish the obstacles in the path of freedom. Not only was he successful, but these same council members now repented and transformed themselves into an honest and selfless committee prepared to serve their previously oppressed people.

One person equivalent to ten persons, and one person equivalent to two persons

Exegetes have written that: "Initially Muslim soldiers were obliged to fight an enemy that was ten times its size. But later on this figure was reduced to two times," based on the following Qur'anic verses:

> Prophet, urge the believers to fight: if there are twenty of you who are steadfast, they will overcome two hundred, and a hundred of you, if steadfast, will overcome a thousand of the disbelievers, for they are people who do not comprehend. But God has lightened your burden for now, knowing that there is weakness in you – a steadfast hundred of you will defeat two hundred and a steadfast thousand of you will defeat two thousand, by God's permission: God is with the steadfast (Q. 65-66).

The tone of these verses is designed to embolden and motivate the soldiers to be patient and persistent when confronting their enemies. The Prophet was commanded to encourage these qualities in his soldiers, for they are essential for defeating the enemy. This encouragement was instituted in two phases: (1) it was postulated that twenty people who were patient, strong, and had a deep understanding of religion would be equivalent to 200 unbelievers who did not possess discernment of religion and had no belief in the hereafter, and (2) it had been postulated that 100 patient and forbearing believers could overpower 200 hostile unbelievers. This latter postulate is a form of a diversified and reduced ratio in the verse in comparison to the ratio of one to ten. However, because it is not so common for one person to overcome ten people, God reduced the ratio to a more likely one to two. For this reason, the following verse says that because He saw some weakness in the Muslim army, He reduced the ratio in order to increase the probability of their success. In summary, these two verses inspire patience and persistence in Muslim soldiers by giving them confidence of victory because their discernment of Islam and belief in God's reward should motivate them to exhibit no weakness. Both military victory and martyrdom would be construed as success and prosperity, which is the outcome of a deep understanding of Islam.

This encouragement and motivation was divided into two phases to indicate that the victory of a patient and religiously committed person with profound understanding of his mission in life over two people who lack these qualities is quite natural and easy to accept. Even the victory of such a person over ten other persons, provided that he has both of these characteristics to a high degree, is not unlikely. But because the Muslims displayed some qualities of weakness, God did not use the ratio of one to ten. Such a concession increases the intensity of encouraging them to aspire for patience and forbearance.

Abrogation of Qur'an, 8:65

Exegetes say:

> In these two verses, the "abstract" (*khabari*)
> sentence gives the meaning of command (*amr*). In
> verse 65, God rules that during jihad one person is
> obliged to stand up against ten of the enemy, but
> verse 66 abrogated this directive and a new ruling
> reduced the ratio to one to two.[71]

Is it possible that God would reveal a mandatory
injunction in one verse and replace it in the immediately
following verse with a new ruling? Was the first
injunction prescribed without any judicious reflection and
thought? Did God immediately understand that this ruling
was not in the public interest and, as such, abrogate it?
We seek refuge in God from those who ascribe such a
thought to Him and say: "This cannot be ascribed to
ordinary legislators, let alone to God, the Wise and the
High!"

In *Tibyan*, Shaykh Tusi writes:

> Verse 66 of *Anfal* abrogates the previous verse
> because the latter had the ratio of one to ten or ten
> to a hundred for someone who is patient and

---

[71] Muhammad b. Hasan al-Tusi, *al-Tibyan fi tafsir al-Qur'an*, ed.
Ahmad Habib al-'Amili (Qum:Maktabah al-a'lam al-Islami, 1988),
5:154; and Muhammad b. Jarir al-Tabari, *Jami' al-bayan 'an ta'wil
ay al-Qur'an* (Beirut: Dar al-fikr, 1994), 10:50-54.

steadfast. God realized that this obligation would be difficult for the Muslims, and, as such, their interest dictated that He reduce this ratio and give them a concession. This statement has been received from Ibn Abbas, Hasan Basri, 'Akramah, Qitadah, Mujahid, Sudda, 'Ata', Balkhi, Jubba'i, Rumani, and all the other exegetes.[72]

It is amazing to observe what kinds of things have been ascribed to the Wise God, and apparently by all the major exegetes: Why would God impose an obligation and, without delay, realize that it would be burdensome and thus immediately abrogate it?! Clearly, making promises and good tidings of victory conditional upon patience and steadfastness cannot be understood as a command and a directive to exercise patience and perseverance. Therefore, one cannot extract from this a religious responsibility (*hukm-e taklifi*). Consequently, we negate the possibility of the verse in question's abrogation, because abrogation does not apply to a report and a promise; rather, it pertains only to those religious obligations which have been implemented for some time.

Unconvincing justification

Some exegetes realized that it was not appropriate to surmise that the two verses were revealed one after another without delay, for if the first verse is prescribing an injunction, then how could the next verse abrogate it

---

[72] Tusi, *Tibyan*, 5:154.

right away? In order to free themselves from this difficulty, the exegetes posited that the second verse was revealed sometime after the first verse.[73]

And because this claim has no proof and is therefore unacceptable, 'Allamah Tabataba'i rejected it and wrote:

> The context of the verses shows that they were both revealed at the same time. However, the implementation of the first verse's injunction is for a time different than that of the second injunction. Thus, these two verses were revealed at the same time but their implementation is related to two different – and therefore separate – times.[74]

This assertion, although not cogent, has been uttered on account of not having an alternative.

It must be underlined that although 'Allamah Tabataba'i argues that there was a time gap between the implementation of the two verses' injunctions, there was no time gap between their revelations. Since he had accepted from the outset that these two verses are prescribing two different religious obligations (*hukm-e taklifi*), he had no choice but to follow this approach. However, if he had not accepted this baseless assertion from the very outset, then he would not have been obligated to justify it with a position that has no basis or evidence. As explained earlier, these two verses do not

---

[73] Ibid., 2:557.
[74] Tabataba'i, *Mizan*, 9:127.

prescribe two different religious obligations; rather, they are examples of a two-phase literary style in which Muslims are encouraged to exercise patience and steadfastness during war, and in which these two phases are connected with each other. Thus, there is no need to embrace the unacceptable justification mentioned in *Majma' al-bayan*, or to accept the justification without proofs introduced by 'Allamah Tabataba'i out of necessity.

Chapter 2

Jihad against Rebels (*Bughat*)

Jihad against rebels (*bughat*), analyzed under the rubric of jihad, is based on the following verse: "If two groups of believers fight (*iqtatalu*), you [believers] should try to reconcile them; if one of them is [clearly] oppressing the other, fight the oppressors until they submit to God's command, then make a just and even-handed reconciliation between the two of them: God loves those who are even-handed" (Q. 49:9).

Important points to consider regarding the verse on rebels (s. *baghi*, pl. *bughat*):

1. In his *al-Kashshaf*, al-Zamakhshari records the following incident as the occasion of revelation for Q. 49:9:

   > The donkey on which the Messenger of God was riding stopped near the place where some Ansaris had gathered for a meeting. The donkey urinated at that spot, and 'Abdallah b. Ubayy covered his nose and expressed his displeasure: "Release your donkey and let it go, as the foul smell bothers us intensely." 'Abdallah b.

Rawahah replied: "I swear by God that the foul smell from the urine of the Prophet's donkey is far more fragrant than the smell of your musk." The Messenger left, but the conversation between the two men continued for some time. Finally, they began fighting. The Aws and Khazraj came and joined in the fight using canes, hands, shoes, and date-tree sticks to beat up each other. The Messenger returned and brought about a truce between them. The verse was revealed at this time.[75]

2. If we accept this assertion, then *iqtital* appears to mean far more than just killing each other. In fact, it includes hitting each other or scuffling. Perhaps the same connotation is conveyed in: "He entered the city, unnoticed by its people, and found two men fighting" (28:15). In this verse, the two individuals were not trying to kill each other, but were embroiled in a scuffle during which many blows were thrown. One of them sought Moses' help, and the latter hit that man's opponent so hard that he died.

3. In its expansive meaning, *iqtital* can be applied to a case in which the enemy has initiated the appropriate preparations with the intent to attack: "The believers are brothers, so make peace (*fa*

---

[75] Mahmud b. 'Umar al-Zamakhshari, *al-Kashshaf*, exegesis on Qur'an, 49:9.

aslihu) between your two brothers" (Q. 49:10). As such, it would be obligatory upon the believers to bring about a truce between the two groups to avoid the outbreak of war, such as when the initial preparations for the battles of the Camel, Siffin, and Nahrawan were underway, but the war had not yet started.

4. This verse contains three directives and commands: (1) bring about a truce through dialogue and any other means that would help restore the relationship; (2) fight against the aggressive party, whose identity would naturally become clear during the peace talks; and (3) seek reconciliation and reparations after the aggressive party retreats and begins to abide by God's law.

Note that in the first and third commands, reconciliation (*islah*) has different meanings. In the first one, it carries the sense of working to end the conflict, but in the third one, it carries the meaning that after the guilty party retreats and signs a peace treaty, it must compensate the oppressed in an equitable manner for the losses incurred. Thus, in this case, *aslihu* is followed by *bi al-'adl* (with fairness) but not so in the first command because it is unnecessary.

5. This verse refers to the internal disputes that sometimes arise within the Muslim community and between countries. Thus, the addressees are Muslim, regardless of whether they are

government officials or people in general. They are warned of their obligation to gather the facts, try to end the war, and compel the wrong party to pay the agreed-upon compensation. All of them are to support this undertaking to the best extent of their ability. Imam 'Ali's letter number 57, as recorded in *Nahj al-balaghah,* contains a poem in which he points out that ordinary citizens must take part in such issues and implement the Qur'anic directives. He wrote this for the people of Kufa when preparing to travel to their city from Madinah to confront the sedition that led to the battle of the Camel in 656:

> Now, I have come out of my city either as an oppressor or as the oppressed, either as a rebel or one against whom rebellion has been committed. In any case, to whomsoever this letter of mine reaches, I appeal to him in the name of Allah that he should come to me and if I am in the right, he should help me; but if I am in the wrong, then he should try to get me to the right according to his view.[76]

As he plainly stated, ordinary citizens are obliged to implement the Qur'an's directives. Basing himself on this duty, the Imam invited them to identify the oppressor and the oppressed and then fulfill their responsibility. Thus, before war breaks

---

[76] *Nahj al-balaghah*, Letter 57, 551.

out, people have to study the position of both sides in order to discern who is in the right and then come to their aid.

6. We can now rationally postulate several scenarios:

    a. Both groups knowingly enter into the battle on unjustifiable grounds.

    b. Both groups believe that it is their religious duty to go to war; however, their decision is based on an ambiguous or incorrect deduction (*ijtihad*), such as that made by the Kharijis.

    c. One is the oppressive group, and the other one enters the battle on the basis of incorrect deduction.

    d. One group is in the right, and the other is in the wrong. The latter group insists on fighting, such as the battles of the Camel and Siffin.

    e. One group is in the right, and the other one initiates the battle on the basis of incorrect deduction, such as the incident at Nahrawan.

In each of these scenarios, Muslims, both individuals and (especially) governments, are responsible for initiating dialogue and other measures designed to prevent war, if it has not yet started. If it has already started, they should strive to bring about a truce and ceasefire through an intelligent and well-thought-out strategy. During the course of these discussions, the true identity of the aggressor and the aggrieved party will become apparent.

Naturally, the aggrieved party would readily accept the suggestion not to go to war or to work out a peace treaty. If the other side agrees not to attack or to suspend a war already underway, then there will be no war. However, if either party refuses to accept the proposal, then the identity of the rebels and the oppressors becomes clear. Once things became clear, the Muslims would have to fight against the latter party until it returns to God's path and repents, or it is completely defeated.

In the first three scenarios, both groups have no justifiable grounds for fighting. If neither of them is prepared to end the war, then both would be regarded as rebels and oppressors. In such a situation, the Muslims would be obliged to fight both groups until they repent or are defeated. If both groups repent, then naturally the war would end, and compensation would be paid to both sides on the basis of equity and fairness. If they do not repent, even then the war would end, because both sides would be subdued and defeated.

7. It is clear from this Qur'anic verse that the aggressive party, which refuses to resolve the dispute justly will be considered the rebellious one. It makes no difference whether these groups are ordinary citizens, if one side is comprised of ordinary citizens and the other is the government, or governmental bodies within the same Muslim country. An example of the latter is Iraq's imposition of war on Iran in 1980. If there was any doubt as to whether the ruler of Iraq is a believer or not, there was no such ambiguity that the soldiers on both sides were Muslim. As a result, this war falls under the rubric of this verse: "If two groups of believers fight" (Q. 49:9). In accordance with the proof of this verse, the oppressive party is categorized as *baghi,* for its wicked nature becomes clear while dialoging with the oppressed party.

This Qur'anic verse is general; however, both Shi'i and Sunni jurists have defined a rebel (*baghi*) as, "the group of people who rebel against the existing government." Their jurisprudential discussion is confined solely to this one definition. Perhaps this is so because such conflicts were often the result of the people being incited against their government, such as those who fought Imam 'Ali in the battles of the Camel, Siffin, and Nahrawan. Other governments have faced similar types of rebellion, whether justified or not, and thus, jurists felt compelled to focus on them and provide legal rulings. The result was the production of a separate chapter/section on rebels (*bughat*) under the rubric of jihad.

Objection

Since the Iran-Iraq war has already entered the discourse, I would like to mention something about it, given that it is related to the verse in question. When the imposed war had just begun, some distinguished Algerians who had good relations with Iran proposed to the chairman of Iran's parliament, who was in Algeria on an official mission, that Algeria serve as a mediator, and in this way initiate a dialogue to restore peace, as required by the Qur'anic directive. They said to the Iranian leader: "God has given a directive in the Qur'an that if two groups of Muslims are embroiled in war, then all Muslims should intervene to bring about peace: 'If two groups of believers fight, you [believers] should try to reconcile them'" (Q. 49:9). The Iranian leader responded: "If it is a war in which neither party is the aggressor, then you would be correct. But if one party is known to be the aggressor, then the Qur'an has made it clear that 'if one of them is [clearly] oppressing the other, fight the oppressors until they submit to God's command'" (Q. 49:9).[77]

Based on this proof and argument, the chairman rejected the proposal and the war continued.

---

[77] Transcript of Majlis-e Shura-ye Islami, 22 January 1980/2 Bahman, 1359.

It is necessary to subject the Iranian's statement to scrutiny and interrogation.

1. His response is open to criticism because the Algerian delegation was proposing to act as a neutral third party to start the dialogue and identify the aggressor. This would facilitate their (Algerian) desire to end the conflict. Their position before the discussion should be one of neutrality because both sides were accusing the other of aggression. As such, the delegation could not identify the guilty party before investigating the issue with fairness and equity. Iran therefore had no right to demand Algeria's support so that Iraq would stop its aggression.

2. The Iranian's assertion that "the aforementioned verse is related to a war in which neither party is the aggressor" is incorrect because, as was demonstrated earlier, the two groups mentioned in this verse could take the form of five different configurations: both sides are fighting an unjust war (the first three forms) and one party is in the right and the other is on the path of excess (the last two forms). This verse applies to all five possibilities.

   The Iranian's position implies that if one or both groups are aggressors, then there is no need to bring about a truce through dialogue and mediation. One cannot glean from the Qur'anic verse that it pertains to a war in which there is no aggressor, because such a situation would mean that Muslims are required to intervene to bring about a truce when neither side is at fault. Clearly, such an interpretation would be no more than an incorrect superimposition.

3. Could there be a war without an aggressor, in the sense that each side was morally justified to act in such a manner? Clearly not, for the aggressor is the one who starts the war. If neither party does so, then there would be no aggressor and, as such, no war. Wherever there is a war, there must be an aggressor. So, the Iranian's statements are not in harmony with reality.

Although it is possible that both parties are aggressors, it is impossible for there to be no aggressor. This is true even if one party is fighting on the basis of incorrect *ijtihad*, such as the Kharijis, who fought Imam 'Ali on the grounds that it was their religious obligation to do so. Such an event is still an aggression, even if they believed themselves to be fighting on the path of truth and therefore not the aggressors. But their false conviction does not alter reality, because transgression was present and the Imam tried his best to prevent the outbreak of war. As the Kharijis ignored his efforts, he had no option other than defense. Their initiation of war is a proof of their aggression.

In any event, the Algerian proposal was an extremely timely and well-intentioned one that was in keeping with the Qur'anic verse. Due to Algeria's good relations with both parties, there was a high probability that it could have established a just peace. This was an opportunity that was lost. Even if the Algerians failed to do so, the ensuing discussion on peace would naturally have circulated worldwide and helped to identify the aggressor. This by itself would have been a victory for Iran, just as the Paris peace talks between Vietnam and the United States helped identify the latter as the aggressor and eventually lead to its defeat and withdrawal.

The Iranian's response, therefore, was illogical and unacceptable, for it constituted an impediment to reaching a possible peace based on justice and equity.

Meaning of *bughat* according to Sunni jurists

The Hanbali school

In his *Mughni*, which is a brief commentary on Kharaki's work, 'Abdallah b. Qudamah (d. 1232) writes: "*Bughat* are a powerful group who, by the use of permitted *ijtihad* and [sound] interpretation, conclude that they are outside the ruler's dominion and are obliged to expel him. The government would attempt to restrain and subdue them."[78]

He defines them in such terms apparently to justify the evil actions of those who supported the battles of the Camel and Siffin, for he and others opined: "All of the Prophet's Companions are just." A religious justification that would rationalize the Companions' rebellion against Imam 'Ali had to be found. The argument chosen was that their *ijtihad* had led them to fight the Imam.

The Hanafi school

'Alauddin Hanafi (d. 1191) defines *bughat* as, "the Kharijis who were steadfast and believed that any sin, whether minor or major, constitutes unbelief (*kufr*). They had rebelled against the just ruler based on their interpretation that every sin is unbelief and, as such, declared war and regarded as lawful the shedding of blood and the disposal of property."[79]

He confines this definition to the Kharijis, probably meaning the Kharijis of Nahrawan, apparently to exonerate the rebels who supported the battles of the Camel and Siffin against Imam 'Ali.

It is not clear why these jurists focus only on historical events, given that the verse on *bughat* is supposed to have

---

[78] 'Abdallah b. Qudamah, *al-Mughni* (Beirut: Dar al-kitabl al-'Arabi, n.d.), 10:49-51.
[79] Abu Bakr b. Mas'ud al-Kashani, *Bada'i' al-sana'i'* (Karachi: Maktabah al-habibiyyah, 1988), 7:140.

perpetual applicability. Why do they not interpret it in a way designed to identify the *bughat* of their own, and of later periods, so that people of every era, until the Day of Judgment, would know their religious obligation regarding them?

'Abd al-Qadir 'Awdah another Hanafi jurist, defined *bughat* as "the ones who transition from obedience to a legitimate imam to an illegitimate one."[80] This definition differs considerably from that of 'Alauddin, perhaps because the latter expressed his own definition, whereas 'Awdah only presented the general Hanafi view.

The Maliki school

'Awdah defines *bughat* in the Maliki school as, "a Muslim sect that disputes with the supreme leader or his deputy in such a way that the right due from them to the ruler [viz., loyalty] is reneged upon or they desire to expel him."[81] Apparently, not giving the ruler the proper right and due has been incorporated to justify the military campaign against those Muslims who refused to pay zakat to Abu Bakr. The reason for mentioning the supreme leader's expulsion is to coordinate it with the protesters who wanted to expel 'Uthman ibn 'Affan.

---

[80] 'Abd al-Qadir 'Awdah, *al-Tashri' al-jina'i* (Beirut: Dar al-Katib al-'Arabi, 1968), 2:673.
[81] Ibid.

The Shafi'i school

'Awdah defines *bughat* in the Shafi'i school as, "Muslims who disagree and dispute with the imam due to the leader's expulsion or not providing him the right that is due to him on the condition that the insurgents have an effective leader who is obeyed, possesses substantial power, and has relied upon interpretation and *ijtihad*."[82]

Meaning of *bughat* according to Shi'i jurists

Shaykh Tusi defines *baghi* as:

> One who rebels against, fights against, and does not render to the just Imam that which is his right and due. *Baghi* is a title of blame and censure (*dhamm*). Some Shi'i scholars believe that *baghi* is an unbeliever (*kafir*); some Sunni scholars agree with this definition. The Mu'tazilis considered *bughat* as wicked (*fasiq*), as did a group among the disciples of Abu Hanifa and Shafi'i. Abu Hanifa has said: "*Bughat* are *fasiq* from the perspective of religion." The companions of Shafi'i have said: "*Baghi*, according to Shafi'i, is not a label for blame and censure; rather, it applies to a person who has performed *ijtihad* but has erred in his deduction, such as the jurists who

---

[82] Ibid.

disagree with each other on matters that warrant *ijtihad*."[83]

It is imperative here to note that Shaykh Tusi uses the term "just ruler" (*Imam 'adil*) to indicate the infallible Imam (*Imam ma'sum*), as he himself stated in many places.[84] The same applies to all Shi'i jurisprudential works where the phrase "empowered Imam" (*Imam mabsut al-yad*), or Imam in the absolute sense is invoked.

'Allamah Hilli, whose *Tadhkirah* contains a chapter on jihad against the *bughat,* asserts: "There is no dispute among Muslims on the necessity to fight the *bughat*." He points out that it is the jurists' customary practice to discuss the Imamate in relation to *bughat* so that the identities of the Imam, who is owed obedience, and the rebel becomes clear. This discussion falls under the discipline of theology, not of jurisprudence.

The following conditions are necessary for the Imam:

1. He has been commissioned or authorized by God,

2. Muslim,

3. Just,

4. Free (not enslaved),

---

[83] Muhammad b. Hasan al-Tusi, *al-Khilaf* (Qum: Mu'assasah al-nashr al-Islami, 1996), 5:335.

[84] Ibid., 3:270, issue 11, 4:189, issue 14, 5:166, issue 28, 5:340, issue 5 and 6:210, issue 2; and Tusi, *Mabsut*, 2:56.

5. Male,

6. Learned (one who knows the legal rulings),

7. Brave and courageous,

8. Competent to give an opinion, and,

9. Ears, eyes, and tongue are sound and free of any ailment.

There is no dissent on any of these.

10. All of his bodily organs and limbs (e.g., hands and feet) must be sound and intact. The Shafi'is also hold this opinion.

11. He must be from the Quraysh, for the Prophet stated: "The Imams are from the Quraysh." This opinion is shared by the Shafi'is; Juwayni, however, objected to it on the grounds that "If someone with the above qualifications cannot be found among the Quraysh, then someone from the Banu Kinana. If this also is not feasible, than someone from the genealogy of Ishmael." This, according to us, is void because we hold that the Imamate is confined to the twelve male descendants of 'Ali and Fatima recognized as Imams by the Twelver Shi'is.

12. According to the Shi'is, the Imam must be infallible because his sole reason for existence is to prevent the Muslims from falling into error, as

this is the source of dissent in society. Given that there is a high probability of rivalry and aspiration to overpower one another, there must be a ruler who is dominant and overwhelming, obeyed, able to execute his directives, and distinguished in excellence from all others. The Imam's appointment should not be left to him or to the people, for doing so allows the likelihood of error. Rather, he should be designated by God and must be infallible. If this were not the case, there would be a need for him to have an Imam to guide him, which would result in an infinite regress. Thus, it is necessary that he be infallible.

13. He must be confirmed by an explicit directive (*nass*) from God, or the Messenger, or by someone else whose Imamate has been established by *nass,* because infallibility is an undisclosed matter which is not something that can be discovered through human debate. If his Imamate is not stipulated in this manner, then human beings would be burdened with a religious obligation beyond their capacity to fulfill.

14. He should be the most meritorious (*afdal*) person of his time.

15. He must refrain from reprehensible things, because infallibility (*'ismah*) demands this. In addition, he must abstain from acts that are viewed as objectionable based on social customs and conventions.

Sunni scholars have contested the conditions from number ten onward.[85]

Two astute and learned questions

We wish to pose two profound questions to 'Allamah Hilli and those jurists who share his opinion:

Question One: Did these jurists consider the obligation of jihad against the *bughat* a perpetual directive, one that is operative as long as Islam exists, or a seasonal one confined to the time of the infallible Imams? If so, it would be limited to the five years and some months rule of Imams 'Ali and Hasan. The condition of infallibility of the leader who fights the *bughat* limits this legal judgment to these two Imams' caliphates, for no subsequent Imam held ever a political office.

Would such jurists accept such a limitation, given that both Imams were infallible, unable to sin, and headed a government? It follows that during the Greater Occultation, one could not find an independent and external case in which to apply this verse and, as such, it would be rendered irrelevant. Is such a claim in harmony with these scholars' grand stature?!

Can these same jurists accept that the ruling proclaimed in this verse would lapse even though its tone indicates an eternal human need for it? If not, they would be obliged to accept the following scenario: If a government such as the

---

[85] Hilli, *Tadhkirah al-fuqaha'*, 1:452-53.

Islamic Republic of Iran, which comes into being during the Greater Occultation due to the people's free choice, is confronted by a group of rebels who declare war on its supreme leader, then all Muslims must work for a peaceful resolution. If one group is determined to be the oppressor, then all Muslims ought to fight it until it returns to God's path. Accordingly, the directive contained in this verse cannot be limited to the period of the presence of the infallible Imam who possesses military power; rather, it remains effective until the Day of Judgment.

Question Two: These jurists have argued that the Imam must be infallible, for it is inevitable that society will fall into error. Thus, there will always be a need for someone to rectify the situation. Are they claiming that the infallible Imam can prevent the occurrence of error in society, or that he would be able to compensate for it and remedy the situation if an error or mistake were to occur? If they are asserting the first viewpoint, then they are mistaken because even during the time of the Prophet and the caliphate of Imam 'Ali, their functionaries were linked to various crimes and acts of treason. For example, after Makkah fell, Khalid b. Walid was entrusted with propagating Islam on the Prophet's behalf. While doing so, he ordered the execution of almost thirty innocent Muslims. The Prophet, greatly disturbed by this horrendous crime, was forced to pay the necessary *diyah* (retaliatory compensation) for all of them:

When the actions of Khalid b. al-Walid reached the Messenger of God, he raised his hands until the whiteness of his armpits were visible saying, "O God, indeed I disclaim to you what Khalid did!" When Khalid arrived, the Prophet censured him...

The Messenger of God said, "... I did not command Khalid to fight. Rather I commanded him to invite them to Islam."

The Messenger of God did not approach Khalid. He turned away from him. Khalid objected before the Messenger of God. He swore he did not kill them for hatred or enmity. But after 'Ali arrived and paid their blood money, the Messenger of God approached Khalid, and continued keeping him among his prominent companions until his death.[86]

Nahj al-balaghah preserves a number of treasonous practices engaged in by 'Ali's functionaries during his caliphate. In the "Letters" section, we find letters number 41 and 71, which represent the harshest reprimand and rebuke against these people.

Letter 41: Now, I had made you a partner in my trust, and made you my chief man. And for me, no other person from my kinsmen was more trustworthy than you in the matter of sympathizing with me, assisting and respecting my trusts. But

---

[86] Waqidi, *Kitab al-maghazi*, 434-35.

when you saw that time had attacked your cousin, the enemy had waged war, the trust of the people was being humiliated, and the whole community was trackless and disunited, you turned your back against your cousin and forsook him when others forsook him, you abandoned him, and you betrayed him when others betrayed him. Thus, you showed no sympathy to your cousin, nor discharged the trust...

Glory be to Allah! Do you not believe in the Day of Judgment, or do you not fear the exaction of account? O you who were counted by us among the men possessed of mind, how can you enjoy food and drink when you know that you are eating the unlawful and drinking the unlawful...

By Allah, even if Hasan and Husayn had done what you did there would have been no leniency with me for them and they could not have won their way with me till I had recovered from them the right and destroyed the wrong produced by their unjust action...Mind yourself and consider for a while as though you had reached the end of life and had been buried under the earth. Then your actions will be presented before you in the place where the oppressor cries, "Alas," while he who wasted his life yearns for return (to the world), "but it was too late to escape" (Q. 38:3)[87]

---

[87] *Nahj al-balaghah*, Letter 41, 511-12.

Letter 71: Now, the good behavior of your father deceived me about you and I thought that you would follow his way and tread in his path. But according to what has reached me about you, you are not giving up following your passions and are not restraining any provision for the next world. You are making this world by ruining your next life, and doing good to your kinsmen by cutting yourself off from religion.

If what has reached me about you is correct, then the camel of your family and the strap of your shoe is better than you. A man with qualities like yours is neither fit for closing a hole in the ground, nor for performing any deed, nor for increasing his position, nor for taking him as a partner in any trust, nor for trusting him against misappropriation. Therefore, proceed to me as soon as this letter of mine reaches you if Allah so wills.[88]

Clearly, neither the Prophet nor the Imam could prevent the occurrence of such crimes.

If these jurists intend to say that the Imam can correct the evil after its occurrence, then this is also doable by one who is not infallible. Accordingly, their proof and argumentation that the Imam and leader of the people must be infallible are defective and fruitless. Moreover,

---

[88] Ibid., Letter 71, 564-65.

they do not resolve the problems faced by contemporary society, which lacks the presence of an infallible Imam.

In any event, this mode of argumentation and proof only produce a self-imposed dead end; the jurists are duty-bound to search for a way out of it. There is no exit from this quagmire, however, other than moving beyond this line of reasoning and searching for a creative solution.

An impossible postulate

'Allamah Hilli and those with a similar opinion state that only the Prophet and the infallible Imams can form a legitimate government. And yet they acknowledge that in their own time no infallible Imam is accessible, because he is in the Greater Occultation. Moreover, they discuss *fiqh* issues which are, in their own words, the exclusive domain of the empowered infallible Imam: offensive war against unbelievers and jihad against *bughat*; making a treaty with unbelievers; obtaining the *jizyah* from the People of the Book and *zakat* from the Muslims; disbursing funds in line with the Qur'anic directive; implementing *hudud* and discretionary punishments as regards murderers, thieves, adulterers, and other criminals; and paying government employees as well as other topics related to the smooth functioning of society. All of these obligations are, according to them, applicable only to the infallible Imam. Thus, one who is not infallible has no right to enter the discourse.

What is the merit of such lengthy discussions and debates, which constitute a major section in evidentiary *fiqh* (*fiqh-*

e istidlali) books (e.g., in-depth political and administrative issues, implementing penal provisions, and economics) if they are all written on the basis of conjecture and supposition? These subjects also consume a good portion of a seminary's budget.

Jurists have laid down a detailed list of responsibilities for the infallible Imam for a scenario that, even according to them, is impossible due to his inaccessibility during the Greater Occultation, and consequent inability to rule. So what is the point of such detailed and rigorous discussions about this person's exclusive responsibilities? Moreover, it appears that jurists are determining his obligations and responsibilities at an enormous cost in terms of time and money, when he himself is obviously capable of figuring out what he is to do when this occultation ends.

Do these jurists mean to say that all of the Qur'anic verses that deal with these legal rulings were revealed exclusively for the short number of years during which the Imams 'Ali and Hasan actually ruled, but then were suspended until the Mahdi's return? Do they mean to say that verses dealing with fighting the unbelievers and *bughat*; paying zakat; matters pertaining to thieves, adulterers, slanderers, and those causing corruption on Earth; consuming usury, and others are to be ignored during the Imam's absence and are only to be recited during prayers and on other occasions to receive reward and divine pleasure?

If one were to accept such assumptions and convictions, the answers to these questions would be "yes."

Perhaps one reason for the stagnancy of Shi'i *fiqh*, especially in matters dealing with government (viz., administering society), is the assertion that only a government led by an infallible ruler can be considered just and legitimate. When such a figure is absent, there is no incentive for jurists to think about how to actually govern and administer a society, or to undertake the fresh *ijtihad* needed for living in the contemporary age. But if a jurist opines that a qualified and deserving person can head a legitimate government by virtue of receiving the people's vote to do so, then naturally all such matters would become operational under his guidance. Thus, there would be an incentive to formulate the necessary rulings and issue progressive *fatwas* designed to resolve contemporary issues by keeping up with the pace of the world. As a result, the stagnancy would end, and people would begin to move toward perfection. If this movement had begun in the time of Shaykh Tusi, by now we would have brought about a grand transformation and progress in the discipline of *fiqh*. Regretfully, this did not occur, and so *fiqh* remained dormant. If it is ever to respond meaningfully to present-day challenges, a comprehensive and serious reexamination is necessary.

Justification of the wrong actions of the *nakithun*[89] and the *qasitun*

Connecting the Hanbali definition of *bughat* with *ta'wil* (subjective interpretation) suggests that the rebels had undertaken *ijtihad* and used it to justify their action. As a result, their action cannot be deemed sinful and immoral because *ijtihad*, even if it produces an incorrect outcome, has religious validation. This interpretation holds true in the case of the Kharijis, because they considered Imam 'Ali an unbeliever and therefore a legitimate (in terms of religious obligation) enemy. But this was not the case with the people who participated in the battles of the Camel and Siffin, because they knew beforehand that their reasons for doing so were illegitimate.

Those Sunni jurists who rely upon the baseless statement that, "All of the Prophet's Companions are just," realized that labeling those who rebelled against Imam 'Ali as *bughat* would not be in harmony with the aforementioned statement regarding the Companions. As such, they introduced the notion of *ta'wil* in order to argue that the participants acted on the basis of their interpretation and *ijtihad*, and thus fought 'Ali out of a sense of religious

---

[89] The three groups are: The ones "who 'broke their covenants' (*al-nakithun*) in disobeying the rightful caliph; those who 'deviated from divine guidance' by raising arms against the righteous government (*al-qasitun*); and those who became 'renegades by seceding' (*al-mariqun*) from the caliph's camp." Abdulaziz A. Sachedina, *The Just Ruler (al-sultan al-'adil) in Shi'ite Islam: The Comprehensive Authority of the Jurist in Imamite Jurisprudence* (New York: Oxford University Press, 1988), 112.

obligation. Accordingly, their quality of justice would not be sullied or ruptured and they would be protected. But what is surprising and unexpected is that Shaykh Tusi mentions this same condition:

> The third condition for the *bughat* is that they separated from the Imam and opposed him based on their interpretation and permissible *ijtihad*. If they had separated from him without engaging in *ta'wil*, then they would be viewed as having cut off their relationship with the Imam, and their judgment would be of one who is a hostile belligerent (*muharib*).[90]

Given that Shaykh Tusi did not regard all Companions as just, there was no need for him to exonerate those who participated in these two battles. However, his position on this matter is identical to that of the Sunnis because he has cited *interpretation* as a condition of *bughat*. How could he justify such a ruling? Perhaps he could do so only because Shi'i and Sunni jurists have always been involved in intellectual and cultural exchanges. Since Sunni jurisprudence dominated the seminaries, it had to have influenced Shi'i jurisprudence to some extent. In this instance, Shaykh Tusi consulted Sunni jurisprudential works and adopted their viewpoint. This reflects the veracity of Ayatullah Boroujerdi's famous statement: "Shi'i jurisprudence is a commentary on Sunni jurisprudence."

---

[90] Tusi, *Mabsut*, 7:265.

Sunni jurists have defined *bughat* in jurisprudential language: "Three conditions are necessary for a group to be labeled as *bughat*: (1) Its members must be organized and of such a numerical strength that they can only be restrained by military force, (2) They are outside the ruler's dominion, (3) They should be able to interpret and perform *ijtihad*."

None of these conditions appear in the Qur'anic verse, which lists only the issues of aggression, reconciliation, and the necessity to fight the aggressor until he returns to God's path. However, jurists have formulated technical terms which they have then employed to discuss and define *bughat*. Perhaps this was done to preserve all of the Companions' probity and integrity because the verse on *bughat* mentions a battle between two groups of Muslims. Quite naturally, this would automatically link and bring to the fore the wars of the Camel, Siffin, and Nahrawan. As a result, Sunni jurists attempted to explain this term in a way that was both historically accurate, and which would protect the Companions' attributes of justice and integrity. In other words, they ignored the fact that the verse's meaning is of a general nature, and does not pertain to any particular event.

Differences in the profile of a *baghi*

Sunni and Shi'i jurists designate a group of people as *baghi* if they rebel against a government. This is a more specialized definition than the general meaning conveyed in the verse. The Shi'i interpretation is even narrower: people who rise up against the infallible Imam's government. Sunnis do not require the ruler to be infallible. In fact, some do not even consider the condition of justice (*'adalat*) to be essential. The Hanbali Ibn Qudamah writes:

> If someone rebels against and overpowers an imam, and then with the force of the sword is able to make the people obey him, then he becomes an imam and any insurgency or warring against him is prohibited. This is based on the evidence that 'Abd al-Malik b. Marwan had rebelled against 'Abdallah b. Zubayr and, after killing him, ruled the lands and its people in such a way that they paid allegiance to him, be it with pleasure or distaste. Thus he became the imam, and rebelling against him was forbidden on the grounds that doing so would create two rival Muslim parties who would shed each other's blood, and cause the loss of their property. Anyone who rose against him would be included in the Prophet's statement: "Whoever secedes from my community while they are all united, sever his head with the sword no matter who this person may be."[91]

Qadi Abu Bakr b. al-'Arabi (d. 1148) holds an opinion similar to that of Ibn Qudamah: "The rise of Husayn against Yazid was an instance of *baghi*, and according to the rulings of Islam, the rebel must be suppressed and punished. As a result, Husayn was killed on the basis of his grandfather's statements." Ibn Khaldun (d. 1406)

---

[91] Ibn Qudamah, *Mughni*, 10:53.

rejected this opinion and argued that the imam who becomes the instrument of crushing the *bughat* must himself be just, whereas Yazid was immoral and wretched and, as such, people should not have fought against Husayn b. 'Ali on the basis of Yazid's directive:

> Likewise, one should not fall into the error of declaring that his [Husayn] murder was justified because (it also) was the result of independent judgment, even if (one grants that) he (on his part) exercised the (correct) independent judgment...It should be known that the matter is not so. The independent judgment of those men did not involve fighting against al-Husayn, even if it involved opposition to his revolt. Yazid and the men around him were the only ones who (actually) fought against (al-Husayn).

> It should be known that only those actions of the wicked are binding that are legal. The (authorities) consider it a condition of fighting evildoers that any such fighting be undertaken with a just ('*adil*) imam. This does not apply to the question under consideration. Thus, it was not permissible to fight against al-Husayn with Yazid or on Yazid's behalf. In matter of fact, (Yazid's fight against al-Husayn) was one of the actions that confirmed his wickedness. Al-Husayn, therefore, was a martyr who will receive his reward. The men around Muhammad who were with Yazid were also right, and they exercised independent judgment [*ijtihad*].

Judge Abu Bakr b. al-'Arabi al-Maliki erred when he made the following statement in his book *al-Qawasim wa-l-'Awasim*: "Al-Husayn was killed according to the law of his grandfather (Muhammad)." Ibn al-'Arabi fell into that error because he overlooked the condition of the "just (*'adil*) imam" which governs the fighting against sectarians.[92]

How wide is the gap between those Shi'i jurists who hold that the Imam must be infallible for one to be called *baghi*, and those Sunni jurists like Ibn Qudamah and Qadi Ibn al-'Arabi, who regard those who rose up against 'Abd al-Malik b. Marwan and Yazid b. Mu'awiyah as *bughat*! This is a clear-cut application of the two extremes of excess and deficiency, neither of which is acceptable. The assertion that the imam has to be infallible is excessive; moreover, there is no proof for it. Shi'i jurists incorrectly conflated the quality of *'adl* (justice), which has been mentioned in the narrations as a condition for the position of imam, with *'ismah* (infallibility).

Ibn Khaldun points out that a person who rebels against a just imam is construed as a *baghi,* but is not so designated if he rebels against an iniquitous imam. This is a balanced position. Based on this criterion, if an armed rebel group rebels against a just leader in the Islamic Republic of Iran,

---

[92] Ibn Khaldun, *The Muqaddimah: An Introduction to History*, trans. Franz Rosenthal (New York: Bollingen Foundation Inc., 2958), 1:446.

then they would be regarded as *bughat* and must be forced to return to God's path.

Is rising against an unjust ruler permissible?

'Awdah writes:

> Even though the notion that justice is a condition for an imam does exist, the more common one among the Sunnis and the Zaydi Shi'is is that rebelling against an oppressive and wicked imam is not permissible even if the intention is to institute the good and forbid the evil (*amr bi al-ma'ruf wa al-nahy 'an al-munkar*). This is because rebelling against a government usually results in the commission of sins and unlawful things that are far greater than the existing situation under the unjust ruler. From this perspective, invoking *amr bi al-ma'ruf* is impermissible because one of its conditions is that the ensuing harm cannot result in something worse than what already exists, such as producing sedition (*fitnah*), shedding blood, spreading corruption, subjecting the citizens to extreme anxiety, misleading the people, losing security, and creating chaos in the government. In principle, people have a right to remove an unjust imam because of his wickedness. But if his removal will cause *fitnah,* then he should not be expelled, according to the jurists.[93]

---

[93] 'Awdah, *Tashri'*, 2:677.

It is worthwhile to probe into the rational principle of "important" (*muhimm*) and "more important" (*ahamm*), invoked by the Sunnis and the Zaydi Shi'is, according to which the "more important" always trumps the "important" due to its superior value and worth. If there is a likelihood of victory, is rebelling against an unjust ruler a superior option compared to the option of not rising up? The answer is "yes"; however, the group must identify the potential benefits and losses, and seek to minimize harm, maximize benefit, and achieve the best possible outcome.

If the likelihood of victory is only probable, due to uncertainty about the outcome and the fact that certain losses can be expected, is it logical to tolerate the harm that is certain in the hopes of attaining that which is probable? Here we need to pay attention to a few points:

1. In a situation where the oppressive ruler is dominant, the harm caused by not rebelling must be measured against the cumulative harm caused by his remaining in power, which will allow him to continue killing innocent people, seizing their property and the public treasury, and destroying the value of spirituality. Not only will those who do not rebel be deprived of a possible victory, but they will also incur an ongoing state of humiliation and loss of their spirituality, property, and life. Such a society will forever be imprisoned by oppressive rulers. Sunni jurists, who prohibit rebelling against such leaders due to their fear of causing harm, are in actuality forcing the people to

tolerate the evils of the oppressor! Is this the right path? Does Islam endorse this?

2. Those who rise up against an unjust ruler to defend themselves are not the aggressors, because it is the oppressor who causes material and spiritual loss, imprisons the public, and sheds innocent blood. By enforcing a culture of suffocation and taking away the people's freedom, he is able to dominate them without any merit and rob them of their basic human rights. Therefore, the insurgent group desires to regain its legal rights and those of the society, both of which have been unlawfully rescinded. This act, which is religiously allowed and praised, is a natural right for each human being.

3. A believer maintains that whatever may be lost in such an uprising, provided that it was undertaken with the best of intentions, will be fully compensated by God. Thus, there is no loss from which he/she cannot recover. A courageous believer and a militant fighter anticipate one of two potential rewards: victory in this world or the prosperity of martyrdom in the hereafter.

4. The group that rises up does so with zeal and enthusiasm to attain victory and continue the struggle, the essence of which is sacred because its goal is to uproot injustice and oppression. If they succeed, they have fulfilled their responsibility; if not, their conscience will be clear when

interrogated by themselves or society because they have fulfilled their moral duty. Thus, they are not the losers in either situation, for God will fully compensate them for their losses, their names will be remembered with pride in historical annals, and they will become dear to their people. This in and of itself is a significant spiritual investment, which the Qur'an calls *lisan sidq*. Prophet Abraham petitions God: "My Lord, grant me wisdom; join me with the righteous; give me a good name (*lisan sidq*) among later generations; make me one of those given the Garden of Bliss —forgive my father, for he is one of those who have gone astray — and do not disgrace me on the Day when all people are resurrected: the Day when neither wealth nor children can help, when the only one who will be saved is the one who comes before God with a heart devoted to Him" (Q. 26:83-89).

The above four positive aspects are present while rebelling against an oppressive ruler, but absent if no action is taken to remove the oppression. Those who are not inclined to rise up assume that doing so will cause more harm and corruption than already exists. Even if this assumption is accurate and their goal is sacred and worthy, without a doubt, its merit can never reach the status of the four positive aspects mentioned above. Thus, the value of rebelling is far greater than that of remaining passive. As such, the former can be categorized as "more important" (*ahamm*) than the latter, especially when the uprising's primary purpose is to liberate Muslims from the ruler's evil motives. The principle of preferring the "more important" over the "important" can be invoked here, as the former always has priority over the latter. Sunni jurists ought to pay close attention to this fact.

Another issue worth exploring is that perhaps the Sunni jurists and the Zaydi Shi'is, who were forced to practice dissimulation (*taqiyyah*) because of intense persecution, were motivated to say: "The famous opinion is not to rise up against an unjust ruler, even if it is under the banner of enjoining the good and forbidding the evil (*amr bi al-ma'ruf wa al-nahy 'an al-munkar*).

The Prophet's hadith vs. the jurists' views

A prophetic hadith, related on the authority of Imam Husayn, directly conflicts with these jurists' opinion. In front of Hurr b. Yazid's army, the Imam proclaimed:

> People, the Apostle of God said: "When anyone sees the authorities make permissible what God had forbidden, violating God's covenant, and opposing the Sunnah of the Apostle of God by acting against the servants of God sinfully and with hostility, when anyone sees all these incidents and does not upbraid them by deed or by word, it is God's decree to make that person subject to the same misfortune." Indeed, these authorities have cleaved to obedience to Satan and have abandoned obedience to the Merciful; they have made corruption visible; they have neglected the punishment (*hudud*) laid down by God; they

have appropriated the *fay'* exclusively to themselves; they have permitted what God has forbidden, and they have forbidden what He has permitted. I have the right to change more than anyone else. Your letters were brought to me, and your messengers came to me with your oath of allegiance that you would not hand me over or desert me. If you fulfill our pledge, you will arrive at true guidance, for I am al-Husayn b. 'Ali, the son of Fatimah, daughter of the Apostle of God. My life is with your lives, my family is with your families. In me you have an ideal model (*uswah*). However, if you will not act, but you break your covenant and renounce your responsibility for the oath of allegiance that you have given, then, by my life, it is not a thing that is unknown of you. You have done that to my father, my brother and my cousin, Muslim. Anyone who was deceived by you would be gullible. Thus have you mistaken your fortune and lost your destiny. For whoever violates his word only violated his own soul. God will enable me to do without you. Peace be with you and the mercy and blessings of God.[94]

Here, Imam Husayn discloses the reason and evidence for his uprising: he was following the Prophet's directive to change the path of the unjust ruler. Would this type of reform movement be labeled an "insurgency" and

[94] Muhammad b. Jarir, al-Tabari, *The History of al-Tabari: The Caliphate of Yazid b. Mu'awiyah*, trans. I. K. A. Howard (Albany, NY: State University of New York, 1990), 19:95-6.

"oppressive," and its participants referred to as *baghi* who, in accordance with Islam, must be killed? Qadi Abu Bakr b. al-'Arabi says: "Husayn was killed on the basis of his grandfather's statements." On what does he base his opinion? What suggestions can the Sunni and Zaydi Shi'i jurists proffer to remove the yoke of oppression when they are inclined to accept the famous prohibition on rebelling against a corrupt and wretched ruler who will not, despite all of their attempts, return to God's path?

If Imam Husayn had managed to set up an Islamic government and rescue Islam and the Muslims from Yazid's oppressive and corruptive influence, he would have replaced the existing suffocation, oppression, and despotism with freedom and justice, as well as the individual's full autonomy and agency. In such a situation, would people like Qadi b. al-'Arabi still say: "He is a *baghi* and an aggressor who deserves to be killed?" Or, is it because Imam Husayn was not militarily victorious and was martyred by an unjust and oppressive government that such scholars seek to rationalize and justify such an act by citing such an opinion?

Necessity of dialogue with the rebels before the start of war

Shaykh Tusi points out that Muslims cannot attack a group that has been declared *bughat* without first having the Imam send his deputy to determine the cause of its displeasure and hostility. If its members are in the right, then their grievances must be handled expeditiously; if their hostility is due to some ambiguity, then efforts must be made to clarify matters. If they then return to a peaceful relationship with the other group, then the objective has been attained. But if they do not do so, then it is imperative to fight them. This approach is based on: "If two groups of believers fight (*iqtatalu*), you [believers] should try to reconcile them; if one of them is [clearly] oppressing the other, fight the oppressors until they submit to God's command, then make a just and even-handed reconciliation between the two of them: God loves those who are even-handed" (Q. 49:9).[95]

A number of points should be noted here:

1. The use of debate and dialogue to prevent the outbreak of war accords with Islam's overarching political mission. Given that Islam views truces as foundational and war as an exception and necessity, both parties are obliged to search for a political resolution of their conflict. If this approach does not resolve the problem, then there is no choice but to declare war. However, even in this situation, the party that is in the right should try to wait for the opponent to initiate the war, for the one who starts the war will be stigmatized as the transgressor and a war-monger. Those who are in the right should not do anything that would cause the people to doubt and become suspicious about the merits of their stand. Imam 'Ali, before the Battle of Siffin began, instructed his companions:

---

[95] Tusi, *Mabsut*, 7:265.

Do not fight them unless they initiate the fighting, because, by the grace of Allah, you are in the right and to leave them till they begin fighting will be another point from your side against them. If, by the will of Allah, the enemy is defeated then do not kill the runner away, do not strike a helpless person, do not finish off the wounded, and do not inflict pain on women...[96]

2. The Qur'anic imperative of reconciling two Muslim groups in conflict applies to all Muslims who have the necessary knowledge, skills, and capacity to do so. Therefore, this undertaking is not confined to the dominant party who has labeled the other group "rebellious." As such, the addressee in "reconcile them" and "fight the oppressors" in the above verse includes the entire Muslim community.

3. What is the rational and legal basis for fighting the *bughat?* At times, the *bughat* reach an incorrect decision, albeit one based on *ijtihad* and *ta'wil*, to rise up against the government. From the Qur'an's perspective, the reason for fighting them does not depend upon a sincere intent (or lack thereof), but rather on this group's transgression against a whole community. A pure intention does not

---

[96] *Nahj al-balaghah*, Letter 14, 473.

change the reality of their transgression or its adverse effects on society.

Chapter 3

The Spoils of War
(*Ghanimah*)

One of the topics discussed in the section of jihad is the spoils of war (*ghanimah*). What is the legal judgment and status of such moveable and non-moveable acquisitions?

What is *ghanimah* (pl. *ghana'im*)?

The root meaning of *ghanimah* is anything that a person acquires. In this regard, Muhammad al-Qurtubi (d. 1273) states: "*Ghanimah* is something acquired by an individual due to his/her own exertion and effort. This is the standard for determining it. That which is taken from the enemy during a war is one type of *ghanimah,* because anything acquired through one's effort constitutes *ghanimah.*"[97]

What is *anfal*?

Nafal (pl. *anfal*) means something that is given to someone. According to linguists: "A meaning of 'additive' has been incorporated into the word's substance." The recommended additional prayers are thus called *nafilah* because they are in addition to the obligatory ritual prayers. The verse, "And We gave him

---

[97] Muhammad b. Ahmad al-Qurtubi, *al-Jami' li ahkam al-Qur'an* (Beirut: Dar ihya al-turath al-'Arabi, 1984), 8:1.

Isaac and Jacob as an additional (*nafilah*) gift, and made each of them righteous" (Q. 21:72) states that God gifted Abraham with a son, Ishmael, due to his supplication, and added sons Isaac and Jacob as *nafilah*.

The spoils of war are also called *anfal* (pl. of *nafilah*) because they are acquired in addition to victory, the ultimate goal. Jungles, pastured and arid lands, and similar items can be labeled *anfal* because they constitute public resources which are in addition to personal fortunes. As such, this term has a general meaning which can be applied to many items, one of which is the spoils of war.

What is *fay'*?

Fay', being a verbal noun (*masdar*) which conveys the meaning of return, applies to anything returned to the Islamic treasury by any means. In sermon 230, Imam 'Ali told his follower 'Abdallah b. Zama'ah, who had asked for some money:

> This money [belongs to the public treasury and therefore] is not meant for me nor for you, but is the collective property of the Muslims (*fay' li al-muslimin*) and the acquisition of their swords. If you had taken part with them in their fighting you would have a share equal to theirs, otherwise the earning of their hands cannot be for other than their mouths."[98] Imam Husayn once rebuked

---

[98] *Nahj al-balaghah*, Sermon 230, 452-53.

Yazid's functionaries "for appropriate[ing] the *fay'* exclusively to themselves.[99]

Clearly, both Imams limited *fay'* to the public treasury.

Refutation of an illusion

Some have imagined that *fay'* is acquired from the enemy without having gone to war and, as a result, have attached this restrictive condition to its meaning. For instance, Shaykh Tusi says in *Tibyan*: "According to 'Ata' b. Sa'ib, Sufyan Thawri, and Shafi'i, *fay'* is something taken from the enemy without going to war." This assertion is also found in the Shi'i hadith collections.[100]

It appears that they based this conclusion on, "You [believers] did not have to spur on your horses or your camels for whatever gains God turned over (*ma afa Allah*) to His Messenger from them. God gives authority to His messengers over whoever He will: God has power over all things" (Q. 59:6). It is assumed that *ma afa' Allah* has been derived from *fay'* and thus linked to the Banu al-Nadir tribe's voluntary abandonment of their homes and lands. From this, they surmised that the condition of "acquired without going to war" is part of this term's meaning. But the reality is somewhat different, because the linguistic meaning of *ma afa' Allah* is "that which is accrued to them and at their disposal." In other words, this

---

[99] Tabari, *The History of al-Tabari*, 96.
[100] Tusi, *Tibyan*, 5:122.

verse cannot be used to define *fay'*, and, as such, this opinion lacks a correct and sound basis.

Kulayni's opinion

Kulayni's opinion is diametrically opposed to the one given by Shaykh Tusi in *Tibyan*: "*Fay'* is something acquired from the enemy during a war." He explains further: "God made the whole world His vicegerent's (*khalifah*) property when He said: 'I am putting a vicegerent on earth'" (Q. 2:30). After Adam, those of his virtuous sons and their successors (the messengers, prophets, and their successors) became the world's owners. Thus the property that reverts back to Adam's virtuous sons and their successors after a military victory is referred to as *fay'* because its lawful owners have regained their possession of it. This legal judgment is also stated in the verse, "Know that one-fifth of whatever you acquire (*ghanimtum*) belongs to God and the Messenger, to close relatives and orphans, and to the needy and traveler, if you believe in God and the revelation" (Q. 8:41).

Kulayni bases his statement on a long and fabricated tradition attributed to Imam 'Ali. Two dishonest transmitters, namely, 'Ali b. Abi Hamza Bata'ini and Hasan b. 'Ali b. Abi Hamzah, are listed in its chain of transmission. One of the issues that impugn their character is their mocking assertion and insistence that the Qur'an has been tampered with, and is therefore no longer extant.

Such hadiths were fabricated due to the excessive love of the Imam's disciples for him, a love that is abnormal and sometimes exhibited even by virtuous and pious people. In fact, *al-Kafi* contains reports which illustrate this excessive love:

> Hadith 1: We found, in the book of 'Ali, peace be upon him: *"Surely, the earth is Allah's and He bequeaths it to whom He will among His servants. The outcome (shall benefit) the God-fearing"* (al-A'raf, 7:128), I and my *Ahlu 'l-Bayt* are those to whom Allah has bequeathed the earth; we are the God-fearing, and the whole earth belongs to us [Ahlu 'l-Bayt].[101]

> Hadith 2: The world and what is in it belongs to Allah, the Blessed, the Sublime, and to His Messenger, and to us [Ahlu 'l-Bayt].[102]

> Hadith 3: I said to Abu 'Abdillah, peace be upon him: "Does *zakat* not belong to the Imam?" He said: "You have phrased the question incorrectly, O Abu Muhammad! Do you not know that this world and the next [all] belong to the Imam, to use in whatever way he wishes, or to give to

---

[101] Muhammad b. Ya'qub b. Ishaq al-Kulayni, *al-Kafi*, translated to English under the supervision of Muhammad Rida al-Ja'fari. (Tehran: WOFIS, 1978--) vol. 1, part three, The Book of Divine Proof (II), 124.

[102] Ibid., 125.

whomever he wishes? He has permission for this from Allah."[103]

Hadith 4: The Messenger of Allah, may Allah bless him and his progeny and preserve them, said: "Allah created Adam, and He gave him the use of the world." Thus whatever belonged to Adam, peace be upon him, belongs to the Messenger of Allah, may Allah bless him and his progeny and preserve them; and whatever belonged to the Messenger of Allah, may Allah bless him and his progeny and preserve them, belongs to the Imams from the Family of Muhammad, peace be upon them.[104]

Kulayni accepted these types of hadiths that the whole world is the Imam's private property without checking its reliability. These exaggerations were then spread by dishonest transmitters and attributed to the infallible Imam. This is calamitous for the corpus of hadith. It is therefore necessary to discredit them, and to delete them from the hadith collections.

This extreme stance that the whole world is the Imam's private property appeared in the latter part of the eighth century CE, and was propagated by such trustworthy people as Ibn Abi 'Umayr. This idea naturally engendered another idea: The act of putting at the Imam's disposal whatever is acquired from the enemy during a war is the

---

[103] Ibid., 127.
[104] Ibid., 130.

moral equivalent of returning the property to its original owner. Thus, it is known as *fay'* with the meaning of "returning."

Neither this nor that

We had mentioned earlier that Imams 'Ali and Husayn applied the term *fay'* to items returned to the public treasury. The linguistic meaning of this term is quite comprehensive, for it encompasses anything returned to the public treasury or the government treasury: sadaqat and zakat, lands obtained via warfare or voluntary submission of their selves and property, taxes levied by the government, and all gains made from other sources (e.g., mines, jungles, and pasture lands). From this, we gather that *fay'* does not mean that which is acquired through warfare (Kulayni), or that which is obtained from not going to war (Shaykh Tusi). Rather, this term can mean anything returned to the public treasury.

Who owns the spoils of war?

Having provided a general definition of *ghanimah*, *anfal* and *fay'*, we now turn to the primary discussion: how Islam views the spoils of war. The first verse to mention this topic also provides a clear ruling: "They ask you [Prophet] about [distributing] the battle gains. Say, 'That is a matter for God and His Messenger, so be conscious of God and make things right between you. Obey God and His Messenger if you are true believers" (Q. 8:1).

Occasion of the verse's revelation

It is related that when the enemy was defeated during the battle of Badr, the Muslims formed into three groups: one chased the fleeing Makkans, another group protected the Prophet, and still another group gathered the spoils. When members of each group realized what was going on, they began arguing. The first group said: "The spoils of war belong to us because we chased the enemy and forced his retreat and flight." Those who had protected the Prophet said: "The spoils of war belong to us because we had surrounded him so the enemy could not assault him in a surprise attack." Those who had collected the spoils of war said: "The spoils belong to us because we gathered it." In this contentious atmosphere, the verse was revealed.[105]

The phrase, "so be conscious of God and make things right between you," reveals the intense disagreement over how to distribute the spoils and calls upon the Muslims to resolve the resulting disputes amicably. The revelation of God's will in this matter effectively settled the disagreement.

It looks quite obvious that this verse was revealed to clear up an entirely new (at least to the Muslims) situation. A hadith from 'Ubadat b. Samit corroborates this: "The verse on *anfal* was revealed regarding us, the people of Badr, when we disagreed in an uncivil manner on how the

---

[105] Qurtubi, *al-Jami'*, 7:360.

spoils of war should be distributed. As a result, God removed it from us and bestowed it upon the Prophet."[106]

Did the verse on *ghanimah* or *khums* abrogate the one on *anfal*?

Most Sunni exegetes have argued that the verse on *ghanimah* or *khums* (Q. 8:41) abrogated the one on *anfal* (Q. 8:1), for they aspire to remove the apparent contradiction between these two formulas of distribution. Consequently, they regard *ghanimah* and *anfal* as synonymous, and translate them as "spoils of war." Qur'an 8:1 (verse on *anfal*) allocates all of it to God and His Messenger, whereas Qur'an 8:41 (verse on *ghanimah* or *khums*) allocates four-fifth of it to the soldiers. Qurtubi explains the resulting conflict:

> Mazari (d. 1141), a Maliki jurist, related this matter on the authority of a large number of Companions: "The imam can distribute the *ghana'im* among the soldiers." To substantiate this edict, he invoked what the Prophet did after Makkah fell, and after the battle of Hunayn." Abu 'Ubayd narrates: "The Prophet overpowered the Makkans and conquered Makkah with his army. He returned the inhabitants' property to them as a magnanimous act and, as a result, did not distribute it among the Muslims as *fay*'."[107]

---

[106] Tabari, *Jami' al-bayan*, 9:172.
[107] Qurtubi, *al-Jami'*, 8:2.

The exact relationship between the verses on *anfal* and *ghanimah* has preoccupied the exegetes, and prompted them to engage in *ijtihad* to find an answer. The ambiguity surrounding these two terms' meanings has resulted in at least one jurist adopting contradictory positions. For example, Shaykh Tusi states in *Mabsut*:

> *Ghanimah* was prohibited in the past for distribution. Instead, God bestowed it exclusively on the Prophet: "They ask you [Prophet] about [distributing] the battle gains. Say, 'That is a matter for God and His Messenger, so be conscious of God and make things right between you. Obey God and His Messenger if you are true believers'" (Q. 8:1). At the beginning, the Prophet used to distribute it among those soldiers who were present, because he had the discretion to do with it as he saw fit. But this judgment was altered and abrogated by the verse, "Know that one-fifth of whatever you acquire (*ghanimtum*) belongs to God and the Messenger, to close relatives and orphans, to the needy and the traveler, if you believe in God and the revelation" (Q. 8:41). Based on consensus (*ijma'*), the soldiers were allotted four-fifths after deducting the fifth part [i.e., *khums*], based on this verse.[108]

---

[108] Tusi, *Mabsut*, 2:25-26.

But in *Tibyan*, his work on Qur'anic exegesis, this same scholar writes:

> Scholars disagree as to whether the *anfal* verse was abrogated or not. Mujahid, 'Ikrimah, Sudda, 'Amir Sha'bi, and Jubba'i have argued that it was abrogated by the *ghanimah* verse, Q. 8:1. Ibn Zayd and Tabari have espoused the view that the *anfal* verse was not abrogated. In my estimation, this second ruling is the correct opinion, because abrogation demands proof. Moreover, there is no contradiction between the *ghanimah* and the *anfal* verses, which would indicate that the former had abrogated the latter.[109]

Shaykh Tusi's ambivalent and conflicting opinions indicate the issue's complexity and the difficulty in resolving it. In fact, he does not explain why he thinks there is no contradiction between them, although he was obliged to do so.

If, as the majority of Sunni exegetes assert, the subject matter of both verses is the same (i.e., it deals with the spoils of war), then the verses would contradict each other: the *anfal* verse puts all the property at the discretion of God and the Prophet, whereas the *ghanimah* verse allocates only two-sixths of the *khums* (i.e., two-sixths of one-fifth of the spoils) to God and the Prophet and its remaining four-sixths to near relatives and orphans, the

---

[109] Tusi, *Tibyan*, 5:73.

destitute and the wayfarers. After deducting the *khums* (one-fifth), the remainder (four-fifths) would have to be apportioned among the soldiers. The fact that these two understandings cannot be reconciled prompted Mujahid, 'Ikrimah, Sudda, Sha'bi, Jubba'i, and also Shaykh Tusi to say in *Mabsut*: "The *ghanimah* verse abrogated the *anfal* verse."

But if the verses' subject matter is considered to be different, then no conflict arises. For instance, if the *ghanimah* verse was revealed about the lawful gains or earnings which one acquires by working, then it would not conflict with the *anfal* verse. If the former verse was not related to the spoils of war, then it indicates an annual 20 percent (one-fifth or *khums*) tax on one's net savings or profit. The infallible Imams unambiguously report that *khums* must be paid on the net profit when it exceeds one's annual living expenses, and that it is to be distributed to deserving recipients every year. One hadith relates that when Imam Abu al-Hasan was asked, "On what items is *khums* obligatory?," he replied: "On every benefit that the people acquire, whether it be small or large."[110]

In a hadith reported on Imam Muhammad Taqi's authority, he received the following written question: "Is *khums* levied on all earnings from every job, be it small or large?" He replied in his own handwriting: "*Khums* applies to all earnings in excess of one's living expenses

---

[110] 'Amili, *Wasa'il al-Shi'ah*, 4:350, hadith no. 6.

for a year."[111] Another hadith relates that he stated, in a letter to his close disciples:

> The one-fifth tax (*khums*) of the *ghanimah* and other gains is obligatory on an annual basis. God has said: "Know that one-fifth of whatever you acquire (*ghanimtum*) belongs to God and the Messenger, to close relatives and orphans, to the needy and the traveler, if you believe in God and the revelation" (Q. 8:41). *Ghana'im* and *fawa'id* are items of value earned or obtained and exchanged among people.[112]

The Imam invokes the *ghanimah* verse to prove that *khums* applies to different kinds of earnings. As such, this verse is not related to the spoils of war, but rather applies to all kinds of earnings. A tax of one-fifth (*khums*) is levied on one's earnings after deducting one's annual living expenses. As such, in these hadiths, *ghana'im* includes all kinds of lawful earnings and has no connection with the spoils of war. The Imam mandates that an annual 20 percent tax (*khums*) be given. In addition, since war is not an annual and inevitable event, this verse cannot possibly apply to its spoils.

The *khums* verse and its ambiguous association

The *ghanimah* verse's placement between the verses on war and jihad results in ambiguity and doubt as to

---

[111] Ibid., 4:348, hadith no. 1.
[112] Ibid., 4:350, hadith no. 5.

whether it pertains to spoils of war, or to earnings and profit in general. Known as the "ambiguous relation," this apparent obscurity is regarded as one of the beauties of speech. For instance, the verse, "The sun and the moon follow their calculated courses; the plants (*najm*) and the trees submit to His designs" (Q. 55:5-6) contains the word *najm*, which, from the linguistic perspective, can be applied to both stars and those plants which have no stem or trunk. The linkage and association between the sun (*shams*) and the moon (*qamar*), which, along with a *najm* (stars), are heavenly bodies which give out light, imply that here *najm* might mean stars. However, this ambiguity is removed by the word trees (*shajar*) coming right after *najm*, which suggests that the latter refers to plants which do not have a solid stem or trunk as opposed to a tree, which has both, to convey the following sense: "Weak plants that do not have a stem or a trunk, along with trees which are sturdy and strong, both prostrate to God in submission." As such, any ambiguity as to the word's meaning is removed.

This ambiguity is also deliberate, because one could easily use *nabt* (plants) for *najm*. But doing so, however, would compromise the verse's beauty and eloquence. The ambiguity is lifted by placing trees (*shajar*) after *najm* to make it categorically clear that *najm* refers to plants, not to stars. Accordingly, here we have both the presence of ambiguity and its subsequent removal. (This delicate use of language naturally could not have been done by an illiterate person without the help and support of an unseen power).

In the *khums* or *ghanimah* verse number 41, this ambiguity is present because verse 39 directs believers to, "fight them until there is no more persecution, and [your] worship is devoted to God alone" (Q. 8:39). Moreover, immediately after the *khums* verse (viz., number 42) the Muslims are reminded of what happened at the Battle of Badr: "Remember when you were on the near side of the valley, and they were on the far side and the caravan was below you" (Q. 8:42). Verse 45 commands them to fight resolutely: "Believers, when you meet a force in battle, stand firm and keep God firmly in mind, so that you may prosper." Positioning the *khums* verse between the verses of war and jihad naturally brings about a degree of ambiguity concerning whether or not it is to be applied to the spoils of war only, or to all gains in general, especially since the verb *ghanimtum* is derived from the same root as *ghanimah* (a possible meaning of which is spoils of war).

This ambiguity can be dispelled by recourse to one's intellect and competent reasoning via reflection, because the ruling in the *anfal* verse is of perpetual relevance. Therefore, the *khums* verse does not need to repeat what has already been explained. Moreover, if *ghanimtum* in the *khums* verse is applied to the spoils of war, then a contradiction would arise between the *khums* and the *anfal* verses. Given this, both in its original and its linguistic sense, *ghanimah* signifies the totality of all gains that a person acquires.

Exegetes who argued that the *khums* verse pertains to the spoils of war failed to pay attention to this "ambiguity of association," which enhances the discourse's beauty. Instead, they interpreted it in the context of war, which resulted in contradiction between the *khums* and the *anfal* verses. In order to resolve this conflict, Qurtubi was forced to contrive a non-cogent and unreasonable stance: the *khums* verse abrogated the *anfal* verse.

In principle, the *anfal* verse, which pertains to public property, cannot be abrogated because acting on its contents is a collective perpetual obligation which must be executed at the discretion of God and His Messenger (i.e., under the guidance of the leader of a society and government), so that it will be disbursed for projects which promote the public welfare. If it were abrogated, how could this occur? Who should manage it properly so that none of it would be wasted? Can one really argue that *anfal* must be left without a custodian? Of course not. Other than the leader of the society, who is also the people's guardian, what other individual or group would be able to manage and allocate this public property appropriately? This question ought to be answered by those who opine that the *anfal* verse was abrogated, for they have implicitly said: "*Anfal* items should not be placed under the discretion of God and the Prophet."

If one desires to untangle himself/herself from this difficulty, then one must abandon the non-justifiable stand and agree that the *anfal* verse was not abrogated, and that it has to be obeyed at all times. Therefore, after the Prophet's demise, it was necessary for a legitimate leader of society to supervise it so that it would have an owner and/or be used to benefit the people.

Jurists did not consider the spoils of war as part of *anfal*

Even though the *anfal* verse was revealed about the spoils of war and considered these items as being under the discretion of God and the Messenger, jurists composed a technical meaning in order to pursue their own reasoning. Here are the opinions of several jurists on this matter.

1. Shaykh Tusi, in *Nihayah* and *Mabsut,* has described *anfal* as follows: Desolate land whose people were overpowered and subdued; land that was not obtained through warfare; land surrendered voluntarily by its owners; mountain tops; the place or cavity where flood waters gather; forests; uncultivated land; the king's palaces and lands, along with his belongings, as long as they are not usurped; the inheritance of someone who does not have an inheritor; the spoils of war before they are distributed (e.g., attractive slave maidens, expensive horses, prestigious clothes, slaves, and luxurious commodities); and war spoils gathered from every war conducted without the Imam's authorization.[113]

---

[113] Tusi, *Nihayah*, 192 and *Mabsut*, 1:263.

2. Abu al-Salah Halabi: Land obtained without engaging in war; land that is a king's exclusive property; uncultivated land; land abandoned by its owner, meaning that he/she makes no use of it (he is the only jurist who holds this opinion); mountain tops; the place or cavity where flood waters gather; the sea, ocean, rivers, lakes, and the like; forests; and estates left behind by those who have no inheritor.[114]

3. Ibn Hamzah writes in *Wasilah* that ten types of *anfal* lands are exclusive to the imam: Land abandoned by the owner; desolate land whose people were overpowered and subdued; land surrendered voluntarily by unbelievers; land that was not conquered due to warfare; uncultivated land that has no owner; forests; mountain tops; the place or cavity where flood waters gather; land appropriated by the king; and land that belonged exclusively to the king, on the condition that it was not usurped.

   The imam possesses the exclusive right to make a judgment on the above lands.[115]

4. Salar b. 'Abd al-'Aziz, in *Marasim*, lists the *anfal* at the imam's discretion: Land that was not

---

[114] Abu al-Salah Halabi, *al-Kafi fi al-fiqh*, ed. Rida Ustadi (Isfahan, Maktabah Amir al-Mu'minin, 1982), 170-71.
[115] Muhammad b. 'Ali b. Babawayh, *al-Jawami' al-fiqhiyyah* (Tehran, n.p., 1860), 681-82.

obtained through warfare; uncultivated and undeveloped land;

the inheritance of a warring unbeliever (he is the only jurist with this opinion); forests; deserts; minerals; and all lands exclusive to the king.

No one has a right to disburse or make use of these items without the imam's permission.[116]

5. Ibn Zuhrah in *Ghunya*, writes that *anfal* consists of: Land surrendered voluntarily by its owner; land abandoned by its owner; land that has no inheritor; the place or cavity where flood water gathers; mountain tops; forests; mountain tops; forests; lands that belonged to the king, so long as they were not usurped; and uncultivated and undeveloped lands.

All of the above are under the imam's exclusive discretion.[117]

6. Shaykh Mufid has enumerated the *anfal* as: Land conquered without going to war; undeveloped and uncultivated lands; the wealth of those who have no inheritor; forests; deserts; minerals; lands that exclusively belong to the king; and waterways.[118]

---

[116] Ibid., 643.
[117] Ibid., 585.
[118] Muhammad b. Hasan al-Tusi, *Tahdhib al-ahkam* (Qum: Dar al-kutub al-Islamiyyah, 1986), 4:132.

These six jurists clearly do not regard the spoils of war as part of *anfal,* even though the *anfal* verse was revealed regarding these very spoils, as attested to by the verse's occasion of revelation. This verse has given God and the Messenger the discretion to do with all spoils of war as they desire. And the latter, being God's representative, naturally can utilize it in whatever way he considers to be in the public's best interest.

Why did these jurists not consider these spoils as part of *anfal*? Shaykh Tusi, Ibn Hamzah, Salar b. 'Abd al-Aziz, and Ibn Zuhrah agree that the infallible Imam has complete discretion over the *anfal*, provided that he has the means and the capacity to govern an Islamic society. This is a sound opinion – in the sense that just as the Messenger had this discretion, after him the infallible Imams had it, and then after them the leaders of the society have had it as well. Thus, until the Day of Judgment they are free to use it in any way that they believe promotes the public interest. Likewise, Shaykh Tusi stated in *Niyahah* that the Imam can let the original owners keep, sell, rent, or utilize it in any other manner which he regards as in the society's best interest, because the Messenger did this as well.[119]

While all of this is accurate and uncontested, one fundamental question remains: Why did these jurists not consider moveable or immoveable war spoils part of *anfal*? Because they obtained the relevant legal ruling from Q. 8:41: "Know that one-fifth of whatever you

---

[119] Tusi, *Nihayah*, 419.

acquire (*ghanimtum*) belongs to God and the Messenger, to close relatives and orphans, to the needy and the traveler, if you believe in God and the revelation" instead of from the *anfal* verse in Q. 8:1: "They ask you [Prophet] about [distributing] the battle gains. Say, 'That is a matter for God and His Messenger, so be conscious of God and make things right between you. Obey God and His Messenger if you are true believers," even though the latter was revealed specifically for these spoils of war.

Shayh Tusi states: "In my opinion, *khums* on the war spoils of non-moveable items like houses, immoveable commodities, and conquered lands must be distributed to the recipients of *khums*. The rest belongs to the Muslims, whether they participated in the war or not. The yield from these items must be used in the Muslims' best interest." However, this contradicts Shafi'i's opinion that the spoils remaining after deducting the *khums* must be allocated only to those soldiers who participated in the war: "The ruling on non-moveable items of war spoils is the same as the moveable, on which *khums* must be levied. The remainder is to be distributed among the soldiers."[120]

Shaykh Tusi clearly deduced his ruling from the *khums* verse, even though prior to its revelation, the *anfal* verse had already rendered an unequivocal judgment. According to this latter verse, no *khums* is to be levied on it, and the soldiers and others have no right to it unless the

---

[120] Tusi, *Khilaf*, 4:194-95.

Messenger or the Imam gives them something in his attempt to promote the public welfare.

If the legal judgment must be deduced from the *khums* verse, then four-fifths of the acquired land must be distributed among the soldiers, just as Shafi'i had said, thereby ignoring Shaykh Tusi's rulings: "Four portions of the *khums* apply to all the Muslims and not just the soldiers," and "Every land that is acquired through warfare belongs to all Muslims, and thus it is not permissible to distribute it among the soldiers."[121] In any event, there is no sound justification for deducing the judgment on war spoils from the *khums* verse, and thereby abandoning the *anfal* verse, as many Sunni and Shi'i jurists have done.

To reiterate, there is no scholarly justification for deducing the ruling on war spoils from the *khums* verse and rescinding the *anfal* verse. In his *Khilaf* and *Mabsut,* Shaykh Tusi regarded the *anfal* verse as abrogated, and yet in his subsequent *Tibyan* he rejected this view.

It is important to note that the hadiths on *anfal*, which constitute the jurists' source of evidence, do not mention anything about the spoils of war. This is not because the infallible Imams did not consider these spoils part of *anfal*, or because they considered the *anfal* verse to have been abrogated; rather, this was done to prevent the reader from being misled into thinking that *anfal* is limited only to the spoils of war. Since these spoils are mentioned in

---

[121] Ibid., 5:534.

the *anfal* verse, there was no need to repeat it again in the hadith literature.

The hadith literature contains only few instances that deal with the spoils of war, for the intent here was to emphasize that only the Imam had any discretion over them. One instance is the *sawafi al-muluk*, the precious things which the kings retain for themselves, and which the Muslims acquire through warfare. Another one is the *qata'i' al-muluk* (land reserved for the kings), and everything which is desirable and valuable which the Imam chooses for himself (e.g., beautiful female slaves, expensive horses, costly clothes, precious swords, distinctive shields, and other such items).[122]

This raises two questions:

Question 1: Given that all spoils of war must be placed at the Prophet's discretion, and after him at that of the Imams, why do the hadiths mention only certain items?

Question 2: Taking into account Imam 'Ali's statement on the leaders' conduct: "Certainly, Allah, the Sublime, has made it obligatory on true leaders that they should maintain themselves at the level of low people so that the poor do not cry over their poverty,"[123] how can the Imam be said to have the first right to claim any of these items? How is it possible to justify or rationalize this, when he is supposed to avoid extravagance and pomposity?

---

[122] 'Amili, *Wasa'il al-Shi'ah*, 4:365, hadith no. 4; 4:372, hadith no. 32; and 4:369, hadith no. 15.
[123] *Nahj al-balaghah*, Sermon 208, 420.

Regarding the first question, one cannot surmise that only those items mentioned in the hadiths are to be placed at the Imam's discretion. Rather, all of the *anfal,* which includes the spoils of war, are to be placed under the Prophet's discretion and, after his death, that of the Imam. This does not mean that they become the items' owners, but only that they are responsible for managing them so that they will be used for the public welfare. The fact that the word *anfal* has a definite article attached to it (*al-anfal*) conveys the sense of totality, namely, that all of it without exception must be disposed of under the discretion of God and the Prophet.

This indisputable legal judgment has been mentioned in the Qur'an's *anfal* verse. How can one reject and overrule this verse, which comes from a source of impeccable authenticity, with certain hadith reports which have a probability of containing both truth and falsehood? It requires a great deal of nerve to place over a Qur'anic verse any hadith that lacks certainty as a proof.

We have a general rule: All hadiths that do not agree with the Qur'an are to be set aside. Those that put only some of the spoils under the discretion of the society's leader conflict with the *anfal* verse, which places all such items under his discretion. Thus, in accordance with this general rule and principle, all such hadiths ought to be disregarded. The correct course is to act upon the *anfal* verse, given its undisputed authenticity.

Regarding the second question, there is no reasonable justification because confining ownership of extravagant and precious items to the Imam is a sign of luxury and indulgence. As this does not conform either to Islam's spirit, or to the Prophet's practice and statements, or to those of the Imams, this opinion is totally unacceptable. Therefore, trying to rationalize them and giving them any credence is pointless, for the net result would be the trumping of an explicit Qur'anic dictate with questionable hadiths.

Appendix

Tension between the Qur'an and Hadith: The Case of Offensive Jihad[*]

HAMID MAVANI

School of Religion, Claremont Graduate University, Claremont, California, USA
hamid.mavani@cgu.edu

ABSTRACT: This paper focuses on the palpable tension between the Qur'anic worldview and the corpus of Hadith literature related to initiating an offensive jihad (*jihad al-talab*) to either proselytize or forcibly convert non-Muslims. I argue that the expansionist theology that could be gleaned from the intolerant *hadith*s was informed by the Muslim community's existing sociopolitical situation and formulated within its concrete experiences during a time when both its territory and hegemony were on the rise. A holistic reading of the Qur'an completely undermines such a position; however, a case can be made for this type of war if one decontextualizes certain verses and then imposes a particular hermeneutics upon them. Given that the Qur'an views freedom of religion and conscience as an inalienable and fundamental right, initiating a war to spread Islam or extend the abode of Islam cannot be justified. Even the sole Qur'anic allowance for war, self-defense, is cancelled once the enemy agrees to a truce and a cessation of hostilities. In other

---

[*] Reprinted from the *Journal of Shi'a Islamic Studies* (JSIS), 4/4 (Autumn 2011), 397-414

words, non-Muslims cannot be attacked just because of their disbelief (*kufr*). Evaluating the juridical and Hadith literature by the standard of the Qur'an often produces results that are diametrically opposed to existing legal judgments not only in the matter of offensive war, but also in such areas as gender equity, apostasy, penal provisions, and minority rights.

KEYWORDS: jihad; offensive war; just war; proselytization; *dar al-Islam*; *dar al-kufr*; *dar al-harb*; freedom of religion; Shahrur, Muhammad; al-Shafi'i, Muhammad ibn Idris.

The term *jihad* conjures up visual images of wild-eyed Muslim zealots riding out of the desert on thundering horses, wielding a sword in one hand and the Qur'an in the other, and enthusiastically seeking to expand the abode of Islam (*dar al-Islam*) by presenting all non-Muslims with the same ultimatum: convert to Islam by reciting the dual testimony of faith contained in the creedal formula or face instant death. The Prophet is reported to have said: 'I am ordered to fight people until they say: "There is no god but Allah"'[1] and 'Every community has a form of asceticism (*rahbaniyyah*), and the asceticism of this community is jihad in the path of Allah.'[2]

---

[1] Muhammad ibn Isma'il, al-Bukhari, *Sahih al-Bukhari*, trans. Muhammad Muhsin Khan IV (New Delhi: Kitab Bhavan, 1980), bk. 52 ('Jihad'), no. 196; IX, bk. 84 ('Dealing with Apostates'), no. 59; and IX, bk. 92 ('Holding Steadfast'), no. 388.

[2] *Rahbaniyyat ummati: al-jihad fi sabil Allah*. This *hadith* is mentioned in both Sunni and Shi'a sources: Ahmad ibn Hanbal, *Musnad Ahmad* (Beirut: Dar al-Sadir, n.d.), 266 and Shaykh Saduq, *al-Amali*

So deeply ingrained is this stereotype that it prompted Godfrey Jansen to assert that 'the image of the Muslim armies converting as they advance has sunk so deeply into the Western mind that no amount of repetition of the truth is likely to dislodge [it].'[3] To counter this stereotypical image, some scholars have advanced the claim that Islam advocates non-violence even in the face of persecution, as this was the norm during the Meccan period of the Prophet's ministry (610-22), when Islam's universal and essential core values were being laid out. During these years he did not resort to warfare, but exercised patience and perseverance. Eventually, he sent some of his followers to Abyssinia and later on migrated (*hijrah*) to Medina.[4]

To further buttress this position, attention is paid to the lexical and etymological meaning of *jihad*: any effort or exertion in a holistic sense – intellectual, religious, physical, spiritual, moral, economical, and psychological – that promotes the public good.[5] Further support is found in those *hadith* reports attributed to the Prophet in which he defines the greater jihad (*al-jihad al-akbar*) as a moral and spiritual striving, an internal jihad in which one combats the moral

---

(Qum: Mu'assasat al-Bi'thah, 1996), 123. See David Cook, *Understanding Jihad* (Berkeley: University of California Press, 2005), 33. Tabataba'i and others have recorded a *hadith* in which asceticism (*rahbaniyyah*) has been equated to migration, jihad, prayers, fasting, hajj, and *'umrah*. Sayyid Muhammad Husayn Tabataba'i, *al-Mizan fi Tafsir al-Qur'an* (Qum: Mu'assasat al-Nashr al-Islami, n.d.), 19:175.

[3] G. H. Jansen, *Militant Islam* (New York: Harper and Row, 1979), 29.

[4] Abdallahi An-Naim, *Toward an Islamic Reformation* (Syracuse University Press, 1990).

[5] For example, *jihad bil-nafs, jihad al-tarbiyyah, jihad al-da'wah, jihad al-lisan, jihad al-qalam*, and *jihad bil-mal*. See Rudolph Peters, *Jihad in Classical and Modern Islam* (Princeton: Markus Wiener Publishers, 1996), 116-18.

vices and evil tendencies present within one's soul.[6] In contrast other scholars, basing their conclusions on a different set of *hadith*s, proclaim that an offensive jihad (*jihad al-talab*) launched to extend the abode of Islam is valid on religious grounds and, moreover, that it is a collective responsibility (*fard kifayah*) devolving upon all Muslims. If it remains unfulfilled, all of them would be guilty of violating a divine injunction. Undertaking this religious obligation is mandated at least once every year and cannot be neglected, as its importance is equal to observing the obligatory prayers, the Ramadan fast, pilgrimage, and giving alms. This suggests that it is incumbent upon every adult male.[7]

These polarized positions are the result of a selective retrieval of textual evidence from the corpus of Islamic literature: the Qur'an, the Hadith (or Sunnah), and the juridical precedents set by eminent historical scholars. In other words, the texts support both theses because they are by their very nature prone to multiple readings, as is the case with practically any scripture. Given the Islamic tradition's

---

[6] John L. Esposito, *Unholy War: Terror in the Name of Islam* (New York: Oxford University Press, 2002), 26-8. J. Cook argues on the contrary that the normative expression of jihad is offensive war and the spiritual jihad against one's self (*nafs*) was derived from the former and not the reverse (Cook, *Understanding Jihad*, 41). The *hadith* on the dichotomy of lesser jihad (military warfare) and larger jihad (*nafs*) was not in circulation until the first half of the ninth century and even then it was found only in the section dealing with asceticism (*zuhd*). In addition, this *hadith* does not appear in the major canonical collections of Hadith (Cook, *Understanding Jihad*, 35). Ayatullah Ruhollah Khomeini views the jihad against the self as a preparatory step to engaging in social activism and transformation in the place of passivity and quietism. Ruhollah Musawi Khomeini, 'Lecture on Supreme Jihad' in *Islam and Revolution*, trans. Hamid Algar (Berkeley: Mizan Press, 1981), 349-62.

[7] Muhammad ibn Hasan al-Tusi, *al-Nihayah* (Beirut: Dar al-Kitab al-'Arabi, 1970), 289.

inherent vibrancy and elasticity on account of being a living tradition, the texts on jihad lend themselves to conflicting interpretations, as is the case with other revelatory texts that mention such issues as the freedom of religion and conscience, apostasy, free will and divine determinism, gender justice, the status of the 'People of the Book' (e.g., Jews, Christians, and Sabeans), the rights of the minorities, religious pluralism, and the Islamic penal code (*hudud*).

This paper argues that the ensuing tension between these two sources, i.e. the Qur'an and the Hadith, at least in the case of jihad, has apparently been resolved in favour of the Hadith literature's overall support for and approval of aggressive jihad. In addition, in my estimation, a cogent case can be made that both Sunni and Shi'a jurists – starting from Imam Shafi'i – relied heavily on the Hadith corpus to formulate their theology of expansionism which, is difficult to sustain based upon the Qur'anic ethos. However, the purview of this paper is confined to the tension between the Qur'an and Hadith, excluding the juridical literature. In this regard, Muhammad Shahrur, a leading Syrian reformist, comments:

> We then realized that the *'ulama*'s interpretations of apostasy, *al-jihad*, and *al-qital* were in fact not too different from the Islamists' positions and that the deviation from the spirit of Allah's *Book* did not just come with the Islamist movement but that it had occurred much earlier in history, namely during the formative period of Islamic scholarship![8]

---

[8] Muhammad Shahrur, *The Qur'an, Morality and Critical Reason: The Essential Muhammad Shahrur*, trans. Andreas Christmann (Leiden: Brill, 2009), 329.

No Compulsion in the Matter of Faith

Muslim jurists of the classical era divided the world into two spheres: the abode of Islam[9] and the abode of unbelief (*dar al-kufr*), war (*dar al-harb*), or polytheism (*dar al-shirk*).[10] The ultimate aim of converting the world to Islam provides an impetus for the Muslim community to remain in a state of ongoing, perpetual, and active state of warfare as it attempts to

---

[9] Shafi'i jurist, 'Ali ibn Muhammad al-Mawardi (d. 1058), defined the abode of Islam in the most expansive manner to constitute the area in which Muslims could openly practice and manifest their religion without any obstacles or harassment. See Khaled Abou El Fadl, 'Islamic Law and Muslim Minorities: The Juristic Discourse on Muslim Minorities from the Second/Eighth to the Eleventh/Seventeenth Centuries', *Islamic Law and Society* I, no. 2 (1994), 150. In contrast, 'Abd al-Walid Muhammad (the grandfather of Ibn Rushd, d. 1122) was the most uncompromising in his stance that it is strictly prohibited for a Muslim to enter or stay in a place where the Muslims are not dominant (*dar al-harb*), idem, 150.

[10] This worldview, conceived at a time when Muslims were the dominant power, eventually had to be modified to accommodate other scenarios, such as religious diversity or Muslims being in the minority. Thus, other intermediate categories were devised: the abode of covenant (*dar al-'ahd*), the abode of peace treaty (*dar al-sulh*), and so on. Also, the notion of safe conduct (*aman*) was introduced to enable the residents in the abode of war to travel into Muslim territory as traders, ambassadors, and visitors. Ibn Taymiyyah (d. 1328), some of whose writings have been removed from their original context and are exploited to legitimize religious extremism, coined the phrase 'the abode of composites' (*murakkab*) to factor in the different religions in his famous fatwa of Mardin. See, also, Yahya Michot, 'Ibn Taymiyya's "New Mardin Fatwa": Is genetically modified Islam (GMI) carcinogenic?', *The Muslim World* CI, no. 2 (April 2011), 130 and *Muslims under Non-Muslim Rule: Ibn Taymiyya on fleeing from sin, kinds of emigration, the status of Mardin (domain of peace/war, domain composite), the conditions for challenging power.* translated, annotated, and presented in relation to six modern readings of the Mardin fatwa (Oxford-London: Interface Publications, 2006).

expand Islam's territory through propagation (*da'wah*) and defeating the unbelievers, for: 'It is He who has sent His Messenger with guidance and the religion of truth, to show that it is above all [other] religions, however much the polytheists may hate this' (9:33).[11]

As such, one could argue that the community's normative state vis-à-vis 'others' is not one of peace treaties and covenants (*sulh*), but of a permanent state of universal war.[12] This transforms war into an essential (rather than accidental) state of the human condition, and peace into a negative peace[13] that is temporary and valued for its instrumental value only to preserve short-term interests.[14] Hostilities can be temporarily suspended, if warranted, out of a serious need or exigency so long as doing so promotes public welfare under the rubric of *maqasid al-shari'ah* (the aims and objectives of Islamic law). Even forced conversion could be regarded as a meritorious act for those stubborn and arrogant unbelievers who either cannot or refuse to discern Islam's truth. As such, at least according to one *hadith*, it is imperative that they be

---

[11] All translations of Qur'anic verses are taken from *The Qur'an: A New Translation*, trans. M. A. S. Abdel Haleem (Oxford: Oxford University Press, 2004).

[12] Patricia Crone, *God's Rule: Government and Islam* (New York: Cambridge University Press, 2004), 362. 'The classical concept of *jihad* is an example, for it is not a mere variant on the ancient Near Eastern idea, but rather a novel conception unique to Islam,' 368. However, there is enough historical evidence to trace the concept of *dar al-sulh* back to the Prophet's time: his signing of a peace treaty with the Christians of Najran when he was in Medina. See '*Dar al-Sulh*' in *Encyclopaedia of Islam* II (Leiden: E. J. Brill, 1960-2005), 131a.

[13] Steven Lee, 'A Positive Concept of Peace', in *The Causes of Quarrel: Essays on Peace, War, and Thomas Hobbes*, ed. Peter Caws (Boston: Beacon Press, 1989), 162-63.

[14] Bassam Tibi, 'War and Peace in Islam', in *The Ethics of War and Peace: Religious and Secular Perspectives* (Princeton: Princeton University Press, 1996), 128-45.

'dragged to Paradise in shackles.'[15]

Although this form of offensive jihad can be convincingly sustained by citing those *hadiths* that praise jihad in the most extravagant terms, it is in direct tension and opposition with the Qur'anic message as regards the freedom of religion and conscience, not to mention those verses that call upon Muslims to stop fighting once the enemy inclines toward peace. Moreover, any faith accepted under duress is without merit and does not entitle the individual to any reward because it would be incompatible with moral responsibility (*taklif*). Abdulaziz Sachedina persuasively argues that his 'categorization of the Qur'anic *jihad* as a "defensive" one is based on the complete absence of any reference in the Qur'an that would justify an "offensive" *jihad*, i.e., a *jihad* undertaken in order to "convert" all of humanity to Islam.'[16]

The Qur'an is categorical that any attempt to impose Islam would be foolhardy and irrational, for one's faith is a matter of one's heart and intellect and thus has to be embraced voluntarily and with conviction. It severely reprimands the nomadic Arabs for their hollow claim that Islam had become anchored in their hearts: 'The desert Arabs say, "We have faith." [O Prophet], tell them, "You do not have faith". What you should say instead is, "We have submitted", for faith has not yet entered your hearts' (49:14).[17] In other words, one's wholehearted acceptance and commitment to Islam is a process that requires full agency and is quite different from

---

[15] Bukhari, *Sahih al-Bukhari* IV, bk. 52 ('Jihad'), no. 254.

[16] Abdulaziz Sachedina, 'The Development of *Jihad* in Islamic Revelation and History', in *Cross, Crescent, and Sword: The Justification and Limitation of War in Western and Islamic Tradition*, ed. James Turner Johnson & John Kelsay (New York: Greenwood Press, 1990), 49, n. 8.

[17] Murtada Mutahhari, 'Jihad in the Qur'an', in *Jihad and Shahadat*, ed. Mehdi Abedi & Gary Legenhausen (Houston: The Institute for Research and Islamic Studies, 1986), 108-9.

the superficial verbal declaration of belief in one God and the Prophet's messengership. Furthermore, the Qur'an censures people who resort to emulation, blind imitation, and sentimental affinity instead of engaging in reflection and proper discernment. It also condemns the Arabs for failing to pay heed to Muhammad's message because of their blind adherence to tribal customs and practices, regardless of their merit or value: 'They say, "We saw our fathers following this tradition, we are guided by their footsteps"' (43:22). Abraham faced a similar impediment during his ministry. When he asked his people what they were worshipping, they replied,

> 'We worship idols, and are constantly in attendance to them.' He asked, 'Do they hear you when you call? Do they help or harm you?' They replied, 'No, but this is what we saw our fathers doing'. (26:72-73)

Various Qur'anic passages point out to Muhammad that human beings have been endowed with the prerogative to either surrender to God and worship Him voluntarily, which is in keeping with their primordial disposition (*fitrah*), or to rise in active rebellion against this inherent tendency in human nature. Rebellion does not impair divine omnipotence, lordship, or sovereignty: 'Had your Lord willed, all the people on earth would have believed. So can you [O Prophet] compel people to believe?' (10:99).[18] Muhammad is advised not to feel disillusioned and despondent at Islam's slow spread in the early years of his prophetic ministry, for he was not entrusted with the forced conversion of his people; instead,

> Your only task is to give warning. You are not there to control them. As for those who turn away and disbelieve, God will inflict the greatest torment

---

[18] Ibid., 101.

upon them. They will finally come to Us, and We shall call them to account. (88:22)

And,

See how We explain Our revelation in various ways, so that they may understand. Yet your people still reject it, even though it is the truth. Say, 'I have not been put in charge of you. Every prophecy has its fixed time to be fulfilled. You will come to realize this.' (6:66)

Moreover, their mocking of the Qur'an and doubting its divine origin also should not worry him:

[O Prophet] are you going to worry yourself to death because they will not believe? If We had wished, We could have sent them down a sign from heaven, at which they would bow their heads in utter humility. (26:3-4)

Imposing Islam would contradict many Qur'anic passages and violate the principles of human agency and free volition, both of which are pervasive Qur'anic themes. Some exegetes have argued that God elevated humanity above the angels because of this free will and designated humanity His deputy and vicegerent (*khalifah*) on Earth to actualize the divine purpose.[19] This freedom of choice provides a basis for the Day of Judgment, at which point God will evaluate every person's actions. The Qur'an reminds everyone that they voluntarily accepted the divine trust, a truly onerous responsibility, after others had shied away from it: 'We offered the trust to the heavens, the earth, and the mountains, yet they refused to

---

[19] Al-Sayyid Muhammad Husayn al-Tabataba'i, *al-Mizan fi Tafsir al-Qur'an*, trans. Sayyid Saeed Akhtar Rizvi (Tehran: WOFIS, 1973), 1:159-70.

undertake it and were afraid of it. Humanity undertook it –
they have always been inept and foolish' (33:72). In addition,
they had entered into a primordial covenant with God before
they were even born:

> [O Prophet,] when your Lord took out the offspring
> from the loins of the Children of Adam [and Eve]
> and made them bear witness about themselves, He
> said, 'Am I not your Lord?' and they replied, 'Yes,
> we bear witness' (7:172).

Ultimately, the decision to accept or reject Islam rests upon
each individual, because God does no more than provide
guidance; He does not coerce anyone: 'We gave him hearing
and sight. We guided him to the right path, whether he was
grateful or not' (76:2-3).

The 'No Compulsion' Verse

An unconditional and explicit verse bestows full autonomy
and discretion upon the individual when it comes to choosing
one's faith: 'There is no compulsion in religion; true guidance
has become distinct from error' (2:256). As such, one cannot
be forced to adopt Islam through intimidation or offensive
warfare; nor can one be deprived of human dignity and equal
rights on the basis of his/her religious faith and conviction.
The choice of religion is a matter of conscience, primordial
nature (*fitrah*), and rational deliberation and thus falls outside
the orbit of compulsion. Allamah Sayyid Muhammad Husayn
Tabataba'i (d. 1981), an eminent Shi'a exegete, represented the
general Shi'a position established from the classical age when
he rejected the use of coercion in the matter of faith and the
abrogation of this verse, which provides for freedom of
religion and conscience:

> In short, religion is belief and faith. It is a matter of

conscience, and such a thing cannot be created by
coercion and compulsion. One may force someone
to do a certain physical action against his will, but
he cannot be forced to believe against his will. Belief
follows reason and understanding, and nothing but
reason and understanding can create it.[20]

Sunni exegete, Muhammad ibn Jarir al-Tabari (d. 923), concurs
that the 'no compulsion verse' has remained operative and
could not be abrogated by later verses, however, he limits the
applicability of this verse to only the People of the Book.[21]
Mahmud al-Zamakhshari (d. 1144), another Sunni exegete with
rationalist proclivities who ascribes to a Mu'tazili theology,
universalizes the applicability of the 'no compulsion verse' to
be inclusive of all human beings because it is part of divine
wisdom to endow everyone with human agency and if He
desired otherwise, He could have forced everyone to become a
believer: 'Had your Lord willed, all the people on earth would
have believed. So can you [Prophet] compel people to believe?'
(10:99).[22]

This verse is generally advanced to refute the claim and
dispel the negative stereotypical image that Islam was spread
by the sword, although many *hadith*s do in fact call for
offensive jihad for the sole purpose of converting non-
Muslims. Advocates of this policy have attempted to blunt the
forcefulness of Qur'an 2:256 by asserting that later (and less
accommodating) verses abrogated and rescinded it; that it
applies only to the protected minorities (*dhimmis*); or that
while it remains operative, the prohibition pertains only to

---

[20] Ibid., 4:171.
[21] Muhammad ibn Jarir al-Tabari, *Jami' al-Bayan fi Tafsir al-Qur'an*,
commentary on 2:256.
[22] Mahmud ibn 'Umar al-Zamakhshari, *al-Kashshaf 'an Haqa'iq
Ghawamid al-Tanzil* (Beirut: Dar al-Kutub al-'Arabi, 1986), 2:372.

the forcible imposition of inner conviction at the esoteric (*batini*) level, as opposed to coercion as regards the outward observances of Islam in the public domain at the exoteric (*zahiri*) level.[23] In addition, the more intolerant Qur'anic verses are given universal currency with general applicability under normal circumstances, while the accommodating verses are circumscribed to be applicable only in exceptional or rare circumstances.

In contrast, 'Allamah Tabataba'i states that this verse cannot be abrogated by the 'sword verse' (9:5) due to its unconditional nature and the fact that the reason cited for the freedom to choose one's religion will always remain valid (i.e., Islam's explicit and clear-cut superiority over all other religions can be rationally ascertained without any force or coercion).[24] Surprisingly, his commentary on the 'jihad verse' in 2:191 explicitly sanctions the use of force against polytheists, which includes the People of the Book, who, in his opinion, are only feigning their belief in monotheism (based on 9:29).[25] He sees no logical inconsistency in claiming that Islam accepts only defensive war while simultaneously championing the cause of conversion not through wisdom, sound proofs, and exhortation, but merely through calling upon the people to convert or face military confrontation. If they accept the invitation there will be no hostilities; but if they decline they will be fought and forcibly converted.[26] This is, after all, not problematic and quite defensible because:

> The compulsion will remain for one generation only. Coming generations will be so taught and trained that they will gladly accept the Religion of

---

[23] Crone, *God's Rule*, 377-82.
[24] Tabataba'i, *al-Mizan*, 4:172-73.
[25] Ibid., 3:95-6.
[26] Ibid., 3:89.

Nature and the creed of the Oneness of God. It is not objectionable if one generation is compelled to see reason, if by that action all coming generations will gladly follow the right path till the end of the world.[27]

Contemporary Muslims can argue that there is little evidence of this expansionist theology in the Qur'an other than general appeals to establish an egalitarian, just, and ethically based public order by commanding the good and forbidding the abominable (*amr bil-ma'ruf wa al-nahy 'an al-munkar*) and providing assistance to those who are suffering under the yoke of oppression.[28] Shafi'i, however, cites such 'unconditional' verses as invitations to engage in offensive wars and elects not to enumerate the conditional verses because, in his estimation, the latter were all abrogated by '[O Believers,] fight them until there is no more persecution' (8:39).[29] If this were the case, then the Prophet's behaviour after his successful conquest of Mecca in 630 would be quite perplexing: he gave immunity to all non-Muslim Meccans who confined themselves to their houses or at mosques and even added the residence of Abu Sufyan, his archenemy, as a place of refuge and protection. It would be nonsensical to provide guarantees of safety if the Meccans had already converted to Islam. No evidence suggests that he forced anyone to convert at the point of a sword. On the contrary, there is

---

[27] Ibid., 3:98.

[28] 'Why should you not fight in God's cause and for those oppressed men, women, and children who cry out, "Lord, rescue us from this town whose people are oppressors! By Your grace, give us a protector and helper!"?' (4:76). The section on *amr bil-ma'ruf and al-nahy 'an al-munkar* is normally classified under 'Jihad' in the books of law.

[29] Muhammad ibn Idris al-Shafi'i, *Mawsu'at al-Imam al-Shafi'i 'al-Kitab al-Umm'*, ed. Ahmad Badr al-Din Hassun (Beirut: Dar al-Qutayba), 5:10.

overwhelming evidence that he told them that they were all free (*tulaqa'*) and bore no responsibility for their past hostility toward the Muslims: 'Go your way for you are the freed ones'.[30]

If the 'no compulsion verse' is considered operative and not superseded by the 'sword verse', then both Sunnis and Shi'as will have to discard, or at least radically reinterpret, the extensive Hadith literature on the mass assault led by the Mahdi or the Messiah, along with Jesus Christ, for the sole purpose of converting everyone so that Islam will triumph over all other religions. It is ironic that many Muslims object strongly to any claim that Islam was spread by the sword, but have no qualms about accepting that these two figures will use force to convert people or about subscribing to the notion that Muslims are obliged to be in a state of permanent war with all non-Muslims. However, this obligation has been suspended until they gain enough strength to resume the campaign of forced conversion (the Sunni view) and the reappearance of the infallible messianic Imam (the Shi'a view).[31]

One also comes across *hadith*s that these figures, who will emerge toward the end of earthly life, will break the cross, kill the swine, demolish churches, and severely reprimand the Christians for deifying Jesus and, as such, will abolish Christianity and summon its followers to embrace Islam: 'By Him in whose Hands my soul is, the son of Mary [Jesus] will shortly descend among you people [Muslims] as a just ruler and will break the cross and kill the pig and abolish the

---

[30] 'Abd al-Malik ibn Hisham, *The Life of Muhammad: A Translation of Ishaq's Sirat Rasul Allah*, trans. Alfred Guillaume (New York: Oxford University Press, 1955), 553.

[31] Majid Khadduri, *War and Peace in the Law of Islam* (Baltimore: John Hopkins Press, 1955), 65.

jizya.[32] Interestingly, these traditions are in direct conflict with those narratives that portray the Mahdi as exhibiting his mastery over all revealed scriptures by judging the adherents of each religion according to their own book: 'He will judge the people of the Torah according to the Torah; the people of the Gospel according to the Gospel; the people of the Psalms in accordance with the Psalms; the people of the Qur'an in accordance with the Qur'an.'[33]

Conditional and Unconditional Verses

There are two types of verses on the issue of jihad: conditional and unconditional. The former establish the limits and conditions for their actualization, whereas the latter are of an absolute nature and thus have no prerequisites or conditions for them to take effect. An example of a conditional verse is: 'Fight in God's cause against those who fight you, but do not overstep the limits. God does not love those who overstep the limits' (2:190) that stands upon its generality. Several of the points made in this verse are worthy of close attention: jihad should be conducted solely with the right intention and for God's pleasure, and not because of any personal or communal desire for vengeance, glory, power, expansion of Muslim territory, or greed for booty. Given that this verse speaks of defending oneself against aggression and subduing the enemy, it is inoperative if the Muslims are not attacked or if the aggressor stops the conflict: 'If they cease hostilities, there can be no [further] hostility, except toward aggressors' (2:193). Consequently, it cannot be invoked to legitimize offensive jihad. Moreover, the imperative form of negation on exceeding the limits (*la ta'tadu*), which is explicit and general

---

[32] Bukhari, *Sahih al-Bukhari* IV, bk. 55 ('Prophets'), no. 657.
[33] Muhammad ibn Ibrahim al-Nu'mani, ed. 'Ali Akbar al-Ghaffari, *Kitab al-Ghaybah* (Tehran: Maktabat al-Saduq, n.d.), 237.

in nature, includes using disproportionate force, harming non-combatants, torching houses, polluting the ecosystem, and all other such excesses. In other words, Muslims have been put on notice not to allow their base tendencies or emotions in the heat of battle to move them beyond the limits set by God, as doing so will engender His displeasure and anger.

Muhammad Shahrur holds that the Qur'an contains overwhelming evidence in support of his thesis that jihad means defending oneself from external aggression, as opposed to offensive warfare for the primary purpose of converting non-Muslims. Jihad has to be distinguished from *ghazwah*, the pre-Islamic practice of launching violent raids against neighboring tribes to acquire booty:

> *Jihad*, originally expressing the notion of self-defence, was finally linked to the offensive concept of 'conquest' through raids (*ghazwa*). This was then retrospectively applied to Muhammad's military actions, which were all identified as 'conquests,' thus contradicting the historical evidence that they were in fact defensive battles of survival (and this includes the battle of Tabuk).[34]

One verse that conveys a similar meaning is:

> A sacred month for a sacred month: violation of sanctity [calls for] fair retribution. So if anyone commits aggression against you, attack him as he attacked you. But be mindful of God and know that He is with those who are mindful of Him (2:194).

This verse was revealed at Hudaybiyyah in 638, when the Meccans prevented the Prophet and his Companions from making the minor pilgrimage to Mecca ('*umrah*) that year.

---

[34] Shahrur, *The Qur'an*, 416.

Here, the Qur'an provides for a proportionate response when fighting one's enemy, even if it be during the sacred month, so long as it is for self-defense. Once again the conflict's scope is defined by the aggressor, because the normal state is that of peace. Proponents of an offensive and aggressive war against the unbelievers, along with those who subscribe to an expansionist theology, declare that this and other verses calling for tolerance were abrogated by verses in Chapter 9, especially: 'But fight the polytheists all together, just as they fight you all together' (9:36).[35] It is hard to sustain this position based on Qur'anic verses and accordingly Tabari asserts that such a stance lacks any sound evidence and constitutes nothing but an illogical and oppressive stance.[36]

Another verse of a restricted (*mahdud* or *muqayyad*) nature is:

> Kill them wherever you encounter them, and drive them out from where they drove you out, for persecution (*fitnah*) is more serious than killing. Do not fight them at the Sacred Mosque unless they fight you there. If they do fight you, kill them, for this is what the disbelievers deserve. But if they stop [fighting within the sacred precincts of Mecca], then God is most forgiving and merciful. (2:191-92).

The chapter's concluding sentence refers to the cessation of hostilities: 'If they cease hostilities there can be no [further] hostility, except toward aggressors' (2:193). Contrary to the interpretation provided by most exegetes, this verse is not a license to annihilate the unbelievers; rather, the context makes it clear that the reference is limited to those Arabs who were belligerent, had expelled the Muslims from Mecca, and who

---

[35] Muhammad ibn Jarir al-Tabari, *Jami' al-Bayan fi Tafsir al-Qur'an*, commentary on 2:190 & 9:36.
[36] Ibid.

had persecuted them in the hope of exterminating both them and their religion, which was still in its infancy.

The conditional nature of this permission to kill is proven by the clause instructing Muslims to end the conflict as soon as the enemy camp agrees to do so. Therefore, this verse can be categorized under 'self-defense.' One may conjecture that the *fitnah* (sedition) referred to in it includes persecuting Mecca's Muslims, driving them out of their homes, plotting and conspiring to weaken the Muslims in Medina by all possible means, and inciting others to fight against them – the sum total of which is considered to be more grievous than killing them, even if this were to take place within the sacred precincts of the Ka'bah.[37]

Two interesting verses on fighting, revealed four years after the first verse that sanctioned jihad, employ the same apparently inflammatory, absolute, unrestricted, and unconditional directive found in the 'sword verse' (9:5). However, here the reference is to the hypocrites (*munafiqun*) who feigned belief in Islam but in actuality had reverted back to polytheism: 'seize [the hypocrites] and kill them wherever you encounter them (*fa-khudhu-hum wa-q-tulu-hum hayth wajadtumu-hum*)' (4:89) and a similar expression in 4:91 with the final phrase '*wajadtumu-hum*' being replaced by '*thaqiftumu-hum*'. Regardless of this difference, it conveys the same meaning. It was revealed in response to the intra-Muslim bickering and dissent on the merits of interceding for those

---

[37] 'Fight them until there is no more *fitnah*' (2:193). Some exegetes have erroneously equated *fitnah* to *shirk* (polytheism) (Tabataba'i, *al-Mizan*, 3:89-90) which suggests that Muslims must engage in offensive war to uproot both polytheism and its adherents. This assertion suffers from two major deficiencies: (1) it is in direct conflict with the 'no compulsion' verse and (2) overpowering the polytheists will not affect their convictions, for this can only be done through dialogue and providing cogent proofs.

considered to be hypocrites. The Qur'an, which censures Muslims for this rancour and divisiveness, advises them to be firm and steadfast in fighting this group. But 'if they withdraw and do not fight you and offer you peace, then God gives you no way against them' (4:90). The unconditional permission to fight is, in actuality, conditional upon the enemy initiating and continuing the attack.

The Evolving Concept of Jihad

Many classical-era Muslim scholars who supported the abrogation of verses dealing with jihad argued in favour of a gradual evolution of this concept – from instructions to exercise patience and perseverance in Mecca via pacifism and non-violent resistance ('[O Prophet], bear everything they say with patience' [50:39]) in the face of oppression and brutality to the culminating unconditional command, revealed in Medina, to 'kill them [the unbelievers] wherever you encounter them' (9:5) to ensure that Islam will triumph over all other religions. One exponent, the eminent Hanafi scholar Muhammad ibn Ahmad ibn Sahl al-Sarakhsi (d. 1090), divided this asserted evolution into four stages:

1. to spread the Islamic Message and Faith peacefully (early Meccan period);

2. to confront and argue with unbelievers in a wise and fair manner (mainly pre-Hijra and early Medinan period);

3. to fight the umma's enemies if Muslims were unjustly wronged, and such fighting was not to be undertaken in the sacred months; and

4. to wage war against unbelievers unconditionally and constantly to bring about the victory of

Islam.[38]

As mentioned earlier, a common strategy employed by some who wished to dispense with the validity of the Qur'an's tolerant and accommodating verses was to argue on the basis of *hadith*s that were in favour of combating disbelief in order to circumscribe the terms of toleration and/or assert that those verses revealed later on, which are of a more belligerent nature and seem to encourage the expansion of Islamdom, superseded the earlier verses. Robert Spencer avers:

> Suras 16, 29, 52, 73, and 109 – the sources of most of the verses of peace and tolerance above – are all Meccan. That means that anything they teach must be considered in light of what was revealed later in Medina (The sole exception to this is the 'no compulsion in religion' verse from the Medinan Sura 2, discussed below.) On the other hand, the last sura revealed, Sura 9, is Medinan. Thus it is in effect the Qur'an's last word on jihad, and all the rest of the book – including the 'tolerant verses' – must be read in its light.[39]

A principle employed to reconcile apparently conflicting verses is that the 'unconditional verses' must be governed and regulated by the restrictions laid out in the 'conditional' verses, instead of arguing that the 'sword verse' abrogated all other verses that deal with jihad. As an illustration, the verse 'So if anyone commits aggression against you, attack him as

---

[38] Quoted in Walter H. Wagner, *Opening the Qur'an: Introducing Islam's Holy Book* (Notre Dame: University of Notre Dame Press), 378 from Richard Bonney, *From Qur'an to Bin Laden* (Houndsmills: Palgave-Macmillan, 2004), 25-7.

[39] Robert Spencer, *Onward Muslim Soldiers: How Jihad Still Threatens America and the West* (Washington, D.C.: Regnery Publishing Inc., 2003), 136.

he attacked you, but be mindful of God' (2:194) reigns over the supposed 'unconditional' verse of 'fight the polytheists all together, just as they fight you all together' (9:36).[40] Thus, initiating an offensive war solely for the sake of converting unbelievers or expanding Islam's territory would be prohibited. In some sense, the conditional verses explain and comment upon the apparently unconditional verses, and the latter are interpreted under the rubric of the former:

> There is a scholastic rule that when both a conditional and an unconditional commandment exist, that is, when there is an instruction that in one place is unconditional but in another place has a condition attached to it, then in the language of the scholars, the unconditional must be interpreted as the conditional.[41]

If this were not the case, many of the verses that have universal applicability and are not subject to abrogation, such as the 'no compulsion' verse and those that instruct Muslims to invite people toward Islam with wisdom, goodly exhortation, and logical arguments (16:125 and 29:46), would be rendered meaningless and irrelevant.

Conclusion

There is tension between the Qur'anic worldview and the Hadith literature as well as between the thematic (*mawdu'i*) and sequential or the verse-by-verse (*musalsal*) reading of the Qur'an in isolation. Those who subscribe to the notion that the corpus of Hadith literature related to initiating offensive jihad gives them a mandate to either proselytize or forcibly

---

[40] Other verses of a similar nature are 2:216, 2:251, 4:74, 4:76, 5:57, 8:24, 9:29, 9:36, 9:123, 21:105, 22:39-40, 24:55, 47:4, and 66:9.
[41] Murtada Mutahhari, 'Jihad in the Qur'an', 95.

convert non-Muslims envision a state of permanent war as a norm until all unbelievers are reduced to non-existence due to conversion to Islam, which implicitly renders Islam a political ideology. Although this position can perhaps be sustained by various *hadith*s, it cannot help but be in direct opposition to the Qur'anic worldview, which explicitly and unconditionally prohibits compulsion in the matter of faith and contains verses that permit fighting only in the case of self-defense, verses that are both restrictive in nature and lack universal applicability. Of additional interest for me is to examine how the juridical literature and the *hadith*s intersect with, are influenced by, and in turn influence the so-called notion of offensive jihad in the Qur'an.

Both Shi'a and Sunni scholars tried to resolve the ensuing tensions and contradictions by resorting to the device of abrogation (*naskh*) or by invoking *hadith*s that had an exclusivistic tone.[42] All verses that are accommodating and tolerant of other faiths and traditions were viewed as having been superseded by the intolerant and exclusive verses, despite the fact this violates a fundamental principle: unconditional verses cannot be abrogated by particularistic ones. Moreover, abrogation pertains only to legal injunctions and thus does not cover such non-legal issues as the freedom of religion and conscience. This profitless undertaking has resulted in 'intellectual dishonesty' or the depiction of a 'new-found politically correct'[43] Islam that resorts to apologetics and

---

[42] 'I submit that it is not only possible to rethink the rationale and consequences of *naskh*, but that it is imperative to do so if we are to resolve the problems raised by the modern application of the public law of Shari'a.' An-Na'im, *Toward an Islamic Reformation*, 21.

[43] Sherman A. Jackson, 'Jihad and the Modern World' VII, no. 1 (2002), 1.

polemics,[44] especially in the aftermath of 9-11, when Islam has been negatively stereotyped as a religion that has a propensity for violence and bloodshed. Such a message pervades the work of Daniel Pipes, Martin Kramer, Robert Spencer, and other scholars.

The process of re-examining the human understanding of Islam's so-called normative and immutable stand on war and peace may be described as a move from a given text to a specific socio-historical context to obtain contextual exegesis. As an extension, the complexity of interpreting a scripture is astutely captured by Vincent Wimbush, who observes that scriptures signify and are signified upon as we make them do what we would like them to do in pursuit of our desired gains in power relations. As such, it would be a fruitful exercise not to confine our analysis to '*what* "scriptures" mean (in terms of content), but [extend our analysis to] *how* "scriptures" mean (in terms of psycho-social-cultural performances and politics).'[45]

In the search for a contextual Islam and an acknowledgment that scriptures signify and are signified upon, Hadith compilations and historical scholarly works should be regarded as tentative and therefore open to scrutiny and reappraisal to prevent time and place-bound human theories and interpretations from being 'absolutized' or given the status of normativity. In other words, these works should not be endowed with an aura of infallibility and timelessness, as if they were somehow formulated in a vacuum and thus

---

[44] This tendency can be found in the publications of various contemporary al-Azhar scholars, for whom 'jihad is a peaceful social struggle against illiteracy, poverty, and disease.' Liyakat Takim, *Journal of Shiʿa Islamic Studies* IV, no. 1 (Winter 2011), 15.

[45] Vincent Wimbush, 'Introduction', in *Theorizing Scriptures: New Critical Orientations to a Cultural Phenomenon*, ed. Vincent Wimbush (New Jersey: Rutgers University Press, 2008), 5.

immune from any socio-historical, political, economic, and cultural influences. Failing to do so would likely allow the Qur'anic worldview on war and peace to be overwhelmed by enabling these all-too-human (and thus limited) works to attain the status of infallibility and sanctification. This would constitute a form of idolatry (*shirk*) and injustice.

The ethos of disputation and difference (*ikhtilaf*) that was so prevalent in historical Muslim scholarship is acutely needed today in order to cultivate cultures of positive and substantive peace, justice, mutual respect and coexistence, harmony, and dialogue. Or, in the words of the Qur'an, a culture of *ta'arafu* (mutual appreciation) and enrichment is needed to create a just and ethically sound social order characterized by inner peace at the individual level and communal peace[46]: 'O people, We created you all from a single man and a single woman, and made you into nations and tribes so that you should get to know one another (*ta'arafu*)' (49:13).

---

[46] 'But God invites [everyone] to the Home of Peace (*dar al-salam*), and guides whoever He will to a straight path' (10:25) and 'those who have faith and whose hearts find peace in the remembrance of God – truly it is in the remembrance of God that hearts find peace' (13:28).

INDEX